# BUILDING POWER, CHANGING LIVES
## *The Story of Virginia Organizing*

By Ruth Berta and Amanda Leonard Pohl

The Prologue first appeared in *Social Policy*, Fall 2015, Volume 45 #3 as
"Roots and Relationships: Reclaiming Community Organizing in the
Obama Era".

Cover design by Mary Wagner
Cover image: Ryan McVay/Getty Images®
Back cover photo by Ben Greenberg

Manufactured in the United States of America
Printed by Bailey Printing, Inc., a family-owned business in
Charlottesville, Virginia


ISBN 978-0-692-45638-5

Virginia Organizing, Inc.
703 Concord Avenue
Charlottesville, Virginia 22903


Social Policy Press
Post Office Box 3924
New Orleans, LA 70177
info@socialpolicy.org

# Dedication

To all the leaders, members, and staff of Virginia Organizing, past, present, and future: thank you for creating a more just Virginia.

# Acknowledgments

We at Virginia Organizing want to express our gratitude to all the individuals and organizations who contributed to the achievements described in this book.

Many thanks to the current Board members for their comments: Sandra A. Cook, Duane Edwards, Debra Grant, Janice "Jay" Johnson, Johnny Mayo, Ladelle McWhorter, Ray Scher, Denise Smith, and Thomasine Wilson.

Thanks, also, to staff members who made helpful suggestions: Addie Alexander, Sally Bastian, Bob Becker, Nik Belanger, Isabel Castillo, Harold Folley, Ben Greenberg, Brian Johns, Michele Mattioli, Maggie Murphy, Laura Ramirez, Teresa Stanley, Joe Szakos, Fancy Terrell, Ben Thacker-Gwaltney, Haley Wilson, and Lauren Wines, as well as to interns Kira Aglio, Madeline Burnham, Yvonne Fox, Jenneca Graber-Grace, Emma Hale, and Edva Kashi.

We used many original sources for this book, written by past staff people, especially Julie Blust, Ellen Ryan, Janice May Sellman, Kevin Simowitz, Steve Vaughan, Cathy Woodson, and Larry Yates.

Virginia Organizing does not keep track of who takes a particular photo. We offer our sincere thanks to all the leaders, volunteers, and staff who took the photos that are used in this book.

Thanks to Heidi Binko and Timothy Pohl for their helpful comments and to Kristin Layng Szakos for copyediting the entire manuscript.

# Preface

**I WROTE THIS BOOK** with Amanda Leonard Pohl, communications coordinator for Virginia Organizing, initially as an internship assignment with Virginia Organizing while I pursued my Master's Degree in Social Work. I love to write and I am fascinated by history, especially the histories of organizations, though I had never written a book before. The story of Virginia Organizing is a living, moving story. My hope is that this book tells a part of that story and helps answer the question, "What does it take to create real change in Virginia?" The book attempts to explain the organizational approach, the Virginia political and social context, and the community organizing lessons that leaders, members, and staff learned over time. We included several appendices so you can read about Virginia Organizing's many, many accomplishments, learn directly from those in the field about building public relationships, and acknowledge the past and current Board members who have committed to the great work over the years.

The sources used to compile the stories are all property of Virginia Organizing unless otherwise noted. I pored over old board minutes and past newsletters so we could retell the story of Virginia Organizing with help from the voices of those who had been there. I hope that this story will contribute to and be remembered as a part of the broader narrative of the people of Virginia and the history of change.

– Ruth Berta, October 2015

*Virginia Organizing was founded as the Virginia Organizing Project (VOP). On the 15th anniversary in 2010, the word "Project" was dropped from the name. The respective name of the organization is generally used in this book as reflected in the time period of the events that are described. The authors often use the term "it" and "its" to refer to Virginia Organizing or VOP. Leaders' voices are more personal.*

# Contents

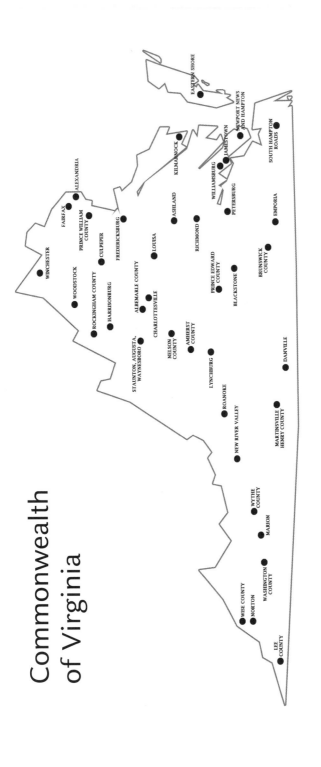

Commonwealth
of Virginia

EASTERN SHORE

NEWPORT NEWS
AND HAMPTON

SOUTH HAMPTON
ROADS

KILMARNOCK

JAMESTOWN

WILLIAMSBURG

PETERSBURG

ASHLAND

EMPORIA

FAIRFAX

ALEXANDRIA

PRINCE WILLIAM
COUNTY

CULPEPER

LOUISA

RICHMOND

FREDERICKSBURG

WINCHESTER

WOODSTOCK

BRUNSWICK
COUNTY

PRINCE EDWARD
COUNTY

BLACKSTONE

ROCKINGHAM COUNTY

HARRISONBURG

ALBEMARLE COUNTY

CHARLOTTESVILLE

AMHERST
COUNTY

STAUNTON, AUGUSTA,
WAYNESBORO

NELSON
COUNTY

DANVILLE

LYNCHBURG

ROANOKE

NEW RIVER VALLEY

MARTINSVILLE
HENRY COUNTY

WYTHE
COUNTY

MARION

WISE COUNTY

WASHINGTON
COUNTY

NORTON

LEE
COUNTY

# Prologue
By Nik Belanger

**"DO YOU KNOW WHERE YOU ARE?"**
The man looked me up and down, shaking his head. I lived a few blocks away and could name every intersection between his house and mine. I had studied the map online for hours. I wasn't lost. But in a very real sense, I didn't know where I was. How could I? I had moved to this new city a few weeks earlier and was just beginning to move beyond the areas you might find in brochures. I didn't know much, but I was determined to learn.

"This is a rough neighborhood," he said. "You can't walk these streets by yourself – it's just too dangerous. You need to leave before something bad happens."

I dug in.

"I'm not going anywhere," I told him. "The problems you're talking about, that's exactly why I'm here. I'm trying to learn more about the community – what people care about and want to see change."

A blank stare. I took a deep breath and asked the question I'd tossed at almost every person I'd met since moving here.

"What do you want to see change in Danville?"

His eyes widened.

"No one's ever asked me that before."

It has been five years since that conversation in early 2010. Since then, I've had hundreds of similar conversations. And here's one thing about which I am certain: the Danville Chapter of Virginia Organizing knows what it means to build power for change. Over the years, we have reached more than 20,000 of Danville's 43,000 residents through door-to-door canvasses, phone banks, and tabling. We have knocked on every door in nearly every low-income neighborhood, many of them multiple times. In July 2014, the Danville Chapter successfully campaigned for the introduction and passage of a Ban the Box resolution to remove criminal history questions from the City of Danville's job applications, overcoming opposition from city staff and reluctance from a few city councilors. We have made thousands of phone calls, trained hundreds and hundreds of community members to take action, and helped people develop their skills as leaders.

And it all grew out of that one question.

While that question – what do you want to see change? – feels second-nature to me now, I realize how foreign it may be for many young organizers today. As the organizer for the Danville Chapter of Virginia Organizing, I am part of a new generation of organizers who joined staffs around the country after the 2008 presidential election. As a former community organizer, the Democratic nominee not only brought the profession to the attention of the general public, but also applied many of its techniques to the campaign itself, and thousands of campaign workers and volunteers learned the power of face-to-face organizing. Along with community organizing's newfound visibility and popularity, however, came a pressure to avoid the grassroots work required to build democratic community organizations. In the years after Barack Obama's first presidential campaign, both intentionally and uncontrollably, the practice of organizing changed in significant ways.

To understand the success of the Danville Chapter of Virginia Organizing today requires an appreciation of its brief history – organized by a young community organizer in the Obama era of mobilization organizing – and the commitment to authentic grassroots organizing that made it possible. What we did in Danville wasn't anything new, but it is increasingly rare in the post-2008 world.

## REAFFIRMING GRASSROOTS ORGANIZING IN THE OBAMA ERA

When I came to Danville in 2010, Southside Virginia was a hotspot on the political map. The Obama campaign had run a successful ground operation to turn out local voters in 2008, but Tom Perriello, the freshman congressman from the president's party, now faced Tea Party backlash and an electoral challenge from a conservative state senator. National groups were pouring resources into the area to influence the election. An environmental issue organizer working on federal carbon tax legislation came to town around the same time I did, while other organizers with various labor, party, and national policy affiliations buzzed in and out of the area.

Following the 2008 election and the legislative possibilities it opened to progressive causes, many advocacy organizations exploited President Obama's short history as a community organizer – and the derisive responses it received from some conservatives – to attract young people to what national legislative advocates called community organizing.

Unfortunately, the issue organizing models in which many of these young adults found themselves looked very different from the grassroots community organizing Barack Obama experienced in 1980s Chicago, where he spent three years organizing residents in one neighborhood. The national issue campaigns parachuted recent college graduates like me into unorganized territory with a script and a demanding list of deliverables in hand. They valued the number of media hits generated, phone banking calls made, doors knocked, and voters registered more than relationships, shared experiences, and leadership development. They looked to mobilize, not organize. In the interest of going fast rather than deep, they engaged people's passion but built little trust and offered no long-term commitment to people in communities or on the organizing staffs.

At a breakneck pace, the environmental organizer in Danville scheduled a community kick-off meeting, set dates for letter-writing parties, organized speakers for campaign events, and got people to take immediate action on the carbon tax issue – with letters, phone calls, and visits to legislators. As best I could tell, the other organizers had similar workloads with even wider territories.

The Danville Chapter was founded in November 2010. Members gathered at this founding meeting to discuss changes they wanted to see in their city.

Virginia Organizing had a different approach. As the parachuted-in organizers rushed from one corner of Southside back to Richmond or Roanoke, my workplan was to ask people what they wanted to see change in their local communities, really listen to their answers, and bring them together to build a local Chapter. My schedule filled with one-to-one conversations, canvassing in communities of color, and small neighborhood meetings. I brought no pre-set agenda and asked no leading questions; in short, I built public relationships, rooted in a shared vision of working together for a better community, with individuals who wanted to see things change.

After Congressman Perriello lost his seat in the 2010 mid-term elections, national groups found themselves without a progressive Representative or a clear agenda to support and largely left Southside Virginia. Four years later, few of the community members who lobbied for carbon cap-and-trade policies remain active in climate change issues. Six months of organizing did not develop lifelong activists or community leaders. Virginia Organizing, on the other hand, still meets on the fourth Tuesday of every month in church basements and fellowship halls, and I'm still asking people what they want to see change in their local communities – and successfully working with them to realize their hopes and dreams.

## GRASSROOTS ORGANIZING AS THE FOUNDATION OF NATIONAL ISSUE WORK

It's easy to imagine how grassroots organizing works to address local problems – street paving, uneven sidewalks, and even overcrowded schools – but can it really affect change on pressing national and global problems? Virginia Organizing's commitment to grassroots organizing has not kept us from considering the "big questions" or precluded effective organizing on national issues. In fact, it has made those efforts even stronger. In my first year in Danville, our State Governing Board and member-led strategy committees, responding to the demands of different national partners and the political moment, would occasionally pass down requests for action to organizers like me. The phrase "only if it makes sense locally" followed nearly every request, as our staff leadership and board sought to keep the focus on local grassroots organizing. By rejecting the national-first approach so common in the Obama era of mobilization-first organizing and instead building authentic relationships, Virginia Organizing has created a core of leaders capable of greater action and ownership at all levels.

Johnny Mayo first heard about Virginia Organizing through a door-to-door canvass in the spring of 2012. Renee Stone, one of our local Chapter members, and a student volunteer from the College of William and Mary were walking through Renee's neighborhood, talking to residents about a city-run weatherization program and asking about their visions for Danville's future. After a good conversation with the canvass team, a friend of Johnny's told him about Virginia Organizing, and they decided to give me a call and set up a meeting to talk more about what they wanted to see change. I spent over an hour at their kitchen table, hearing stories of harassment and systemic racism within the City of Danville Police Department. Rarely did a month pass where Johnny or one of his friends did not have an encounter with the police, and they felt frustrated that nothing had changed.

"We're in the middle of a different local campaign right now," I explained, "but we should keep this on our list for the future." As the conversation went on, I talked about the organizing process and how one victory builds for the next victory. That approach made sense to Johnny, and he started working on the Chapter's active weatherization campaign, meeting with city councilors and learning more about the strategy. In small ways at first, Johnny was building power for change, working on a variety of local and statewide Virginia Organizing issues.

But my conversations with Johnny didn't stop there. About a month later, Virginia Organizing decided to make a coordinated push on Senator Mark Warner's office. After months of unsuccessfully jumping through hoops to schedule a meeting with Senator Warner to discuss Social Security, a news story broke that he was on a budget retreat at a posh West Virginia resort. Our State Governing Board had had enough. Organizers started looking for members to write pointed, critical letters-to-the-editor about Senator Warner's willingness to cut Social Security benefits for future generations and his unresponsiveness to the concerns of everyday Virginians. I worked with Johnny to help him write and publish one of those letters, and for whatever reason, his letter caught the attention of Mark Warner's staff. Tell them to stop, Senator Warner's staff told us.

A few weeks later, Johnny was on the way to Washington, D.C. After writing a letter to the editor critical of Senator Warner's position on Social Security, he was invited by our State Governing Board to participate in a meeting with Senator Warner. Alongside people with dozens of years of experience, this brand new member met with a national decision-maker. Sandra A. Cook, the Board chairperson, scheduled reflection time after the meeting and talked with Johnny about his experience. From a conversation around a kitchen table about a local police department, this resident of Danville was helping to influence policy at a national level. Johnny is now on the State Governing Board himself and has represented Virginia Organizing on the board of a national partner organization.

But most importantly, with all of his new experience on statewide and national campaigns, Johnny's focus remained on building power locally. The following spring, the Danville Chapter researched discriminatory policing and began working to develop local partnerships to address the issue. Johnny spoke as a panelist at a community forum, met with the chief of police, and talked with friends about the problem. Rather than redirect Johnny's energy away from this local issue to a national campaign, I made sure that he – and our whole Chapter – built a foundation locally. It's a lot easier for people to connect to national issues from the bottom up once the base is established than it is to fill in the base from the top down.

Johnny Mayo's story is not all that rare in community organizing. In my first few years organizing in Danville, I met people where they were and kept myself focused on what they wanted to see change in their communities. By learning about power in a local

Danville Chapter leader and State Governing Board member Johnny Mayo holds a city proclamation honoring Virginia Organizing's 20th anniversary.

context – police departments, school districts, and even neighborhood associations – community members became more capable participants in national campaigns as both activists and strategists. Paradoxically, it was Virginia Organizing's commitment to the local-first approach that made us such an effective partner on these national issue campaigns.

## EFFECTIVE ORGANIZING REQUIRES MORE THAN PASSION AND PROCESS; IT REQUIRES COMMITMENT

Before I joined the staff of Virginia Organizing, I was an active member of its Williamsburg Chapter. Thanks to a local organizer and experienced leaders who spent time sharing stories and ideas with me, I had a decent grasp of the organizing process. But I didn't understand what it took to build a strong local Chapter, especially for a new organizer in a new place.

When I signed my contract to become Virginia Organizing's staff organizer in Danville, our executive director told me that I shouldn't bother unless I was willing to dedicate at least five years.

For a recent college graduate, five years can feel like a long time. Few of my friends have spent more than two years in one place. Peace Corps, Teach for America, consulting firms, and large non-profits cater to a "don't sit still" mentality that encourages young people to develop a wide array of experiences and neglect long-term commitment. A friend who works as a research-focused consultant in Washington, D.C., became a manager after proving her dedication to the company and gaining seniority by staying in place for an entire 12 months, after many of her coworkers left for grad school or moved to other cities.

In my first months in Danville, in addition to regular canvassing, I worked through the usual suspects for one-to-one conversations: local labor union leaders, community college instructors, social service providers, and religious leaders, among others. In one conversation, I sat down across the desk from a staff person at Danville Community College. We talked about her passion for education, the effect of state budget cuts on the community college system, and what it was like working with students. When I asked her if she'd be interested in meeting with some other community members who also care about education, she shook her head.

"If you're still here in six months, give me a call."

Our conversation was not the first time she'd sat down with a new organizer. She wasn't going to invest her time in an organization that wouldn't invest its time in her community.

A couple years later, I shared this story with Pastor Loretta Murray, one of the leaders in the Danville Chapter, and asked her why she stuck with us over the years.

"I wasn't sure who you were or what Virginia Organizing was all about when we first met," she said. "But when I saw where you lived, I knew you weren't going anywhere anytime soon. I could tell you cared."

When I moved to Danville, I chose to live in one of the poorer communities of color – a choice, without a doubt, made possible by my privilege. I bought an old, abandoned house for under $12,000 and spent every paycheck and every hour of free time fixing it up. For Pastor Murray, that personal choice I made conveyed an important message. Before we developed a Chapter in Danville, I was the face of Virginia Organizing, and she could tell that Virginia Organizing cared about her community. To become effective community organizers, new staff members need to commit – not just to an issue or organization, but also to a place.

The relationship is not one-sided, though. Organizations must also make commitments to their new organizers. I arrived in Danville a brand new organizer with only a couple years of experience as a local Chapter member and intern. Experienced organizers – people who had been in the fight for 30 years and had won major campaigns – invested time in my development, helping me to analyze and understand this new community. Another young staff organizer, a recent college graduate who cut his teeth on a university living wage campaign and now worked with a local Chapter over three hours away, called every day to help me through those tough first months organizing in a new place. We cannot expect new organizers to pick this up on their own. Good organizing requires good training, and it takes at least two years to understand the basics of community organizing well enough to apply them consistently. To create capable young organizers – and strong organizations for the future – trainers and supervisors need to commit to their new organizers.

In my first year on the job, not only did I receive guidance from my new colleagues, but Virginia Organizing also provided me with the opportunity to attend a Midwest Academy "Organizing for Social Change" weeklong training in Baltimore. Virginia Organizing gives staff five days of paid time and a $500 stipend each year for self-development. Over the years, I've used these resources to read and learn more organizing history, visit other organizations, and attend gatherings of organizers. By devoting the time of experienced organizers and the resources for me to learn on my own, Virginia Organizing made it possible for me to commit to them.

Now five years in, I'm able to make good on the investment that Virginia Organizing made in me by taking on more responsibility within the organization. I staff a planning committee to organize our annual statewide meeting with seasoned leaders from across the state. I work with other organizers on questions of leadership development and facilitate exchanges between leaders of different Chapters to share ideas and experiences. These and other opportunities have allowed me both to think about bigger organizational questions and to continue to learn new skills. In turn, I realized that I have a role to play in helping other organizers who are just starting out find their place in this work and commit to it for the long haul. Without demanding this kind of dedication, the progressive movement will not build power. Organizations will face rapid turnover and burnout, and new organizers will lack the grounding to face a challenging responsibility. Young organizers must open themselves up to deep commitment, and grassroots organizations must respond by providing the support to make that possible. Organizations, organizers, leaders, and members grow stronger through commitment – when we really are all in this together.

And here's the hard truth in the Obama era of mass mobilization organizing: short-term, issue-specific mobilizing does not provide opportunities for that kind of commitment. Strong community organizations can and should mobilize, but it must be grounded in leadership and organizational development – in other words, from the grassroots up. Members of the Danville Chapter have called legislators, organized demonstrations on national issues, and registered voters, but only when it makes strategic sense to our leaders and builds for long-term change. When national groups send new organizers into the field with a laser focus on the passage of a piece of legislation, it's hard to see purpose beyond that specific vote. And when organizers bounce from one group to another every six months, it's hard for the organizations to justify any real investment in their growth. To sustain organizers and build strong organizations, we need to develop longer timelines, with space for transformative relationships.

For new organizers to find purpose in this work, we need the freedom to build meaningful relationships without the constant pressure of mobilization deliverables.

In the spring of 2007, I became a member of Virginia Organizing not because the Williamsburg Chapter organizer asked me to phone bank, sign an online petition, or execute a small part of a preplanned action. I got involved because he invited me to learn about issues that mattered to me, participate in meetings with local elected officials, and develop creative tactics. He was not constrained by deliverables but was instead able to engage me in the organizing process in a more organic, meaningful way.

Deliverables – the metrics by which national networks and funders often measure an organization's success – should reflect what matters most in community organizing. Canvassing, one-to-one conversations, house parties, and leadership trainings are more indicative of effective organizing than what many organizers today have to report, like phone banking calls, earned media, ghostwritten letters, and social media followers. To build strong community organizations capable of making long-term change, organizers and organizations should be measured by the things that will make long-term change possible – the building blocks of strong public relationships.

Community members signed up to take action during the North Main Hill Community Meeting in Danville in 2011.

## DEEP RELATIONSHIPS MAKE A DIFFERENCE

Five years in, it's not the excitement of a protest or the novelty of meeting with a politician that keeps me going; instead, it's the deep relationships that I have developed with people whose lives and opinions matter and who are directly affected by decisions made by public officials. Relationships provide not only a source of personal fulfillment but also a strong foundation for community organizing.

I first met Ernest Williams while canvassing in his neighborhood on the south side of the city. When I asked him what he wanted to see change in his community, he complained that the young men in the neighborhood played their music too loud. We talked for a few more minutes about how long he'd been in his neighborhood, the people who lived there, and what it was like growing up in Danville some 60 years ago.

Over the next two months, Ernest and I saw each other at least once a week. We talked about the civil rights movement in Danville and what Vietnam was like – he had experienced both. He would save some leftovers for me if he knew I was coming by late. When his brother passed away, I dropped off a meal for him and his wife. As we built a relationship, he started coming to a our small planning meetings at the public library, participated in a Dismantling Racism Workshop, and introduced me to the families who lived in his apartment complex. I learned that loud music wasn't really his top concern but that he hadn't really thought about being able to change bigger problems before.

From this and other conversations, a group of Virginia Organizing members decided to ask the Danville City Council to endorse a federal job creation bill. This decision grew out of our desire for action and seemed like a no-brainer in a city with double-digit unemployment. We collected petition signatures, held a rally in Ernest's neighborhood, and submitted letters to the editor. Ernest published an op-ed in the local newspaper and even spoke at a City Council meeting about the need for jobs in his city. We were ready for a win. However, at their work session, City Council turned us down. One council member told us that people wouldn't work anyway now that they were all getting checks from the government. We lost. It felt like the getting the wind knocked out of us. We left there defeated.

The following week, Ernest called me late one night.

"Nik, we need more white people in the group," Ernest said. "If we want to win, we need to be diverse. When City Council looks at us and sees that you're the only white face in the crowd, they just write us off. We need some of everybody if we want to win."

Over the next few months, I spent more time canvassing in low-income white communities, learning about white churches and charities, and revisiting supportive white folks I had met along the way. Ernest continued talking with his friends and neighbors – mostly people of color – and, together with several other dedicated leaders, we built a truly diverse Chapter. The Danville Chapter still isn't a perfect reflection of our community, but Ernest helped move us a lot closer to that goal.

My relationship with Ernest not only gave me purpose but also provided insight into our organizing process when I needed it most. Had I met Ernest and immediately asked him to sign a petition or attend a rally, we would be strangers today – and the Danville Chapter would have a very different story to tell. Had Virginia Organizing dropped me in a new place with a weekly quota for phone calls or media events, I don't think I'd still be organizing today. If we believe that relationships provide the foundation for effective organizing, we must recommit ourselves to an organizing approach that places a high value on their development.

For organizations to take full advantage of new organizers' passions, they need the resources to make five-year commitments possible – regardless of election results or shifts in the national campaigns.

I moved to Danville at a particular national political moment. Health care reform was near-reality. Virginia was suddenly an important place to D.C. dealmakers, with momentum from the Obama victory and two moderate senators. In 2009, it was an easy decision to put someone in Southside Virginia – and resources flowed to make that happen. By the end of 2010, however, many national funders decided that money could be better spent in some other political hotspot. While many of the issue organizers moved to more populated parts of the state or quit organizing altogether, I was left out there by myself.

This funding shift – a decision made in Washington, D.C., and other faraway places – could have meant the end of my time in Danville as it did for other organizers. Thanks to Virginia Organizing's strong web of grassroots donations, major donors, and some supportive foundations, I never had to worry about being sent to Virginia Beach, Fairfax County, or the Richmond suburbs. Both the organization and the organizer honored their commitments – to each other and to the community.

When organizations rely too heavily on short-term grants and contracts, they forfeit the ability to make strategic decisions. In the Obama era, funding has flowed for mobilization work and issue campaigns, not for base-building and leadership development. Strategy is left to experts at the national level, and organizers become executors of plans. While this approach might work in the short term, national funders simply do not share the same commitment to a community that a grassroots organization does. The funding cuts that might accompany the retirement of a key congressman or a sudden shift in policy can force organizations to abandon communities and leave organizers out of work.

In order to protect themselves from the lure of quick cash, community organizations must raise their own money and build partnerships with like-minded funders. Supportive funders, in turn, must provide multi-year grants to organizations to make long-term commitments possible. Virginia Organizing does not rely on funding tied to the changing winds of national campaigns and foundations. Through careful strategic planning and incremental growth, the State Governing Board has consistently valued long-term commitments in its budget. If more organizations could make the same investment that Virginia Organizing made in me, we would have a stronger pool of young organizers working in communities to build power and make change across the country.

## SO WHERE DO WE GO FROM HERE?

In 2015, we are at a crossroads, and my generation of social justice organizers will either dig in or check out. Now is the time to reclaim community organizing as a distinct practice apart from mobilization-first issue organizing. In the Obama era of organizing, despite the pressures to move away from the grassroots, community organizing continues to represent our best hope for change.

As a new generation of organizers, we can commit ourselves to living in local communities, building relationships, training leaders, and making change. It won't get the most likes, retweets, or shares. It will be hard to explain to our friends and family. But we will have deeper relationships than we thought possible and something to be proud of.

We know what we need to win: it's time to trade our parachutes and scripts for roots and relationships.

# Introduction

**IN THE MID-1990S,** Denise Smith was living in Southwest Virginia. Through her own life experience, she saw firsthand – being homeless, fighting for her husband's disability claim, struggling to get student loans for college – that social and economic change was needed in Virginia. When she tried to call for change, she felt ignored by state elected officials and policymakers who didn't seem to pay attention to people from her part of the state. A professor she knew from her college days, Dr. Steve Fisher, told her about a community organizer named Joe who might have an idea about how to effect real change in Virginia. She decided to hear what he had to say.

Denise met Joe Szakos at McDonald's in Wytheville, a small town in Southwest Virginia that is closer to the capitals of North Carolina and West Virginia than it is to Richmond. Joe had moved from Eastern Kentucky to Charlottesville, Virginia, so he and his wife could raise their children in a more diverse community. With Joe's experience as a community organizer and Virginia's long history of injustice, an idea was born.

"I knew this was something different, something real," Denise remembers now, "and I wanted to be a part of it."

Virginia Organizing's history has grown over the past 20 years in much the same way it began: with grassroots organizers living and working in communities, talking with the people who are most deeply affected by poverty, injustice, racism, classism, sexism, heterosexism, and other forms of oppression. By reaching out to people one by one and building relationships, Virginia Organizing starts with the assumption that people with real lived experiences are the experts of their own circumstances.

That was the goal in that first meeting with Denise – to learn from her about her life in Bland County and to see if she was interested in changing her community and state. When Denise and Joe met, she told him she was tired of "legislators pretending Virginia ends at Roanoke." While there were organizations doing good work in Southwest Virginia at the time, no one was consciously organizing people to build power and create long-term change. Denise tells everyone who will listen that she really did not know what she was getting into:

Denise Smith (holding microphone) spoke at the 15th anniversary celebration in 2010 about local victories in Southwest Virginia. Jay Johnson, the State Governing Board Chairperson at the time, held a poster illustration.

*When we began the Virginia Organizing Project, there were all these different people who did not know each other. From the very beginning, VOP included people from all across Virginia, of all races, genders, ages, sexual orientations, faiths, political parties, and abilities coming together to figure out how to create a statewide organization to change what we all agreed needed to be changed in Virginia. Joe Szakos brought us all together and helped us to start building relationships in our communities so we could create this statewide organization. He had every single one of us attending Dismantling Racism workshops, attending meetings together in different locations, and breaking down barriers with each other before we worked on breaking down barriers in the state. Each one of us came to it at a different time in our lives and with a different view, really.*

*I had never championed LGBT issues or race issues – I had never done community organizing like this! Even though I am a heterosexual white woman, I, and the rest of the Organizing Committee, understood that those issues were critical if we wanted to build what we really wanted – even if it looked a little radical at the time. I learned from meeting all these different people that the problems and issues across the state are so similar and affect all of us.*

*I eventually found myself sending letters to the editor, meeting legislators, and writing to policymakers about issues affecting people and communities not my own but all over the state. Because even though our communities are separate on the state map, we have a common need to see Virginia succeed for all of us, and for those in power to represent all of us.*

*It's different when you get to know people who are directly affected. The Virginia Organizing Project was a unique and new way to start creating change in our state by bringing diverse people to the table. It was – and still is – different, and it works.*

Virginia Organizing has been able to address problems where people live and where change can have lasting consequences. Certainly in 1995 there were issues that needed to be addressed in other parts of the Commonwealth, but it was clear that Southwest Virginians were largely ignored and needed a catalyst for raising their collective voice and taking action on the issues unique to people of the area. This commitment to people who are traditionally silenced shows a belief in the value of all people, no matter how far away from the state capital they may live, or how economically challenged the area may be. People of color, people with disabilities, people who identify as gay, lesbian, bisexual, transsexual, or genderqueer, people with lower incomes, and others are all empowered to take action on issues that matter to them in a way that honors their dignity and respects their individual and collective voices. These are the people who make up Virginia Organizing. Virginia Organizing works hard not to speak *for* anyone, and avoids being labeled as an "advocacy group" that works on behalf of others. Instead, Virginia Organizing works alongside individuals to amplify individual and community voices and work together for change.

## STAYING TRUE TO ITS ROOTS

While the organization has worked on some state and national issue campaigns as it grew, Virginia Organizing has never lost touch with its original roots – real people raising their voices and taking action to create real change in their communities. In 2014, when the political climate in the Virginia legislature and Congress was very divisive and not as ripe for policy change, Virginia Organizing shifted to a more concentrated focus on local and non-legislative issues. This shift resulted in more victories and new energy – two important components of grassroots community organizing. The focus on local campaigns and leadership development increased the depth of work that could make a big difference in the lives of people directly affected in the here and now.

The national and state legislative work remained an important, albeit smaller, component of the organization as Virginia Organizing became more deliberate about which campaigns to undertake. When the U.S. House of Representatives leadership refused to allow a vote on an immigration bill that included a path to citizenship and would have likely passed a House floor vote, State Governing Board members and other Chapter leaders were arrested in solidarity with immigrant youth in Washington, D.C., calling for reform in the legislative process. At the state level, pushing for expansion of Medicaid under the Affordable Care Act, Virginia Organizing Chapters amped up the pressure on Virginia state senators and delegates in their home districts by holding vigils and community forums, encouraging local people to submit their opinions to editors of newspapers, making visits to legislators' offices, and more. The Fredericksburg Chapter even delivered a homemade coffin to Speaker of the Virginia House of Delegates William Howell's district office to symbolize the people who would die that year in Virginia without Medicaid expansion.

It is 2015 as this history goes to press, and Denise Smith is still working toward the change she envisioned in that meeting 20 years ago. In 2012, she had to resign from her job due to severe medical problems. Although she was able to get disability benefits, she continues to be concerned about health care because members of her family are not getting the medical attention they need due to Virginia's failure to expand Medicaid. She is also passionate about protecting Virginia's natural resources, increasing diversity in elected leadership, and expanding voting rights and access. Denise, like other long-time Virginia Organizing leaders and supporters, understands that sustainable long-term change takes time to accomplish. It is slow, it is incremental, but it is lasting.

When long-term change feels far away, it can be tempting to start looking for shortcuts and quick fixes. Denise's experience has convinced her that in order for change to last beyond one rally, one piece of legislation, one generation, the organization must build a base of leaders willing to work together through thick and thin. Virginia Organizing remains committed to the communities and the constituencies who have been ignored or dismissed by those in power. The organization has extended its reach to all corners of Virginia: from Virginia Beach to Harrisonburg, Fredericksburg to Danville, Petersburg to Pennington Gap, and all points in between. New chapters are being organized each year. The staff has grown to 20, with 13 full-time community organizers and plans for more in the coming years.

Virginia Organizing will keep working until all voices are heard and Virginia is a fair, equitable, and just place for all people. This 20-year history tells the story of how Virginia Organizing has made progress toward that goal and how we plan to build on this work to create an even stronger future.

This history book is truly just the beginning of the story. Virginia Organizing is developing new relationships every single day to raise the voices of directly affected people to build more power and change oppressive structures in Virginia. The organization is growing by hiring new, diverse community organizers, raising more funds from grassroots supporters, moving into new communities, and building strong partnerships for expanding work on children's issues, climate change, and women's issues. Virginia Organizing will continue to adapt and embrace new technology, while staying true to grassroots organizing models that value people taking action, developing more Chapters, and recruiting and supporting new local leaders.

Denise Smith and the other leaders who have become part of Virginia Organizing are real people, working for real change in their communities. In Virginia, that's a big deal.

# CHAPTER 1

# Getting Started

*Virginia has a long history of inequality. For generations, slaves fueled the engine of the Virginia economy, producing tobacco to sustain the lavish lifestyle of white plantation owners. Poor Virginians have always lived in the shadow of great wealth, their needs overshadowed by the desires of the wealthy, often conservative elite.*

*But Virginia was also the cradle of American democracy, the place where it was first argued that all citizens should participate in the decisions that affect their lives. It was a Virginian, Thomas Jefferson – a slaveowner, ironically – who so ably argued that citizens whose interests are not represented by those in power have a duty to take charge of their own destiny. It is this heritage that the Virginia Organizing Project is determined to reclaim.*

**DUG UP FROM** the archives in the Concord Avenue office in Charlottesville, Virginia, the above statement from an early foundation grant proposal provokes thoughts on Virginia's unique history and Virginia Organizing's remarkable vision for a more just Virginia. How is a statewide, non-partisan, grassroots organizing, non-profit organization reclaiming American democracy? Let's start at the beginning.

Virginia Organizing Project's first organizer, Joe Szakos, brought together three original incorporators – Steve Fisher, John McCutcheon, and David Rubinstein – to file the organization's incorporation papers and jump through a few other "bureaucratic hoops" like creating financial and personnel policies, opening bank accounts, and getting state approval for non-profit fundraising. Szakos had come to Virginia after 12 years as the Coordinator of the statewide group Kentuckians For The Commonwealth, and wanted to see if it was possible to create an organizing model to meet the unique needs and history of Virginia and its people.

From July 1994 to August 1995, logging more than 40,000 miles on Virginia's highways and small back roads, Szakos conducted more than 250 one-to-one meetings with concerned Virginians across the state and learned that there was no grassroots, multi-issue, social change-oriented organization in Virginia. From these meetings, Szakos also learned that Virginians faced a myriad of problems: a lack of jobs, tense race relations, poor workers' compensation and welfare policies, environmental threats, barriers to small business development, a lack of investment in infrastructure like roads and bridges, rising utility rates, a shortage of affordable housing, a lack of access to health care, consumer issues, an antiquated tax system, difficulties with voter registration, a lack of transparency in government ethics – and the list went on.

Out of those 250-plus conversations, Szakos learned some important lessons from early VOP leaders. Margaret Morton and Jill Carson told story after story about rampant racism. Steve Powell raised serious concerns about how lesbian, gay, bisexual, and transgender Virginians were treated in terms of employment, housing, and accommodations. Debra Whitaker talked about the challenges of living in public housing with a husband who is disabled and caring for their five children.

Andy Kegley lamented that the joy when local residents had stopped one private prison from being built in Wythe County was completely overtaken by the sad news that another prison would be built in Brunswick County. "We sent that prison to a low-income African-American community," Andy said regretfully. "With a statewide group, we would have had a chance to warn other communities about these dangerous proposals."

In the years prior to the formation of the Virginia Organizing Project, there had been dramatic shifts in national policy focus from the federal to the state level – a process known as "devolution." This was due to efforts to decentralize the federal government by placing more power and respon-sibility in the hands of the state governments. Whereas before, national organizations could work on policy issues at the national level, now every state legislature was a potential battlefield on every issue. As this shift happened, there were very few resources available to assist existing local community groups, to help to organize new statewide groups, or to get com-munities to work together at a state level. VOP could help to fill these gaps in organizing in Virginia. VOP would encourage citizen participation and could work to build a statewide power base, grounded in local communities and made up of local people – real grassroots.

Based on his findings, Szakos wrote an initial assessment summa-rizing his conversations with people from across Virginia and noted,

"Unfortunately, there is no multi-issue grassroots organization in Virginia that encourages the active participation of its members. There is a great deal of potential and that's what we would like to explore. This is Virginia, not Michigan or Montana or Missouri or Mississippi. We need to figure out what will work here. We need to look at what models of community organizing are working in the '90s, and see what can be applied in Virginia."

Another conclusion Szakos reached from his conversations was, "Most current statewide organizations in Virginia are single issue, do not feel that they are effective, think it would be great to involve more grassroots people, but have no sound plan for doing so... Most staff people for these organizations are advocates, not organizers." While Virginia Organizing still believes that advocates are important and that it takes a lot of different people and groups to get things accomplished, the lack of community organizing in Virginia meant that there were people in the state whose lives were being affected by bad policies who had little to no say in the decision-making process. Grassroots community organizing was vital because, when done well, it empowers people to go beyond storytelling and move into action to create lasting change in their communities and in their own lives.

In addition, he wrote, "There is a need for a statewide organization that has systems of multiple leadership (reducing domination by one person or persons, including staff), democratic decision-making, sound planning and evaluation, and accountability."

A key observation of the initial assessment was very direct: "One of the most important questions of all is: How can different races work together in Virginia on a pro-active agenda? Instead of always being against something, the organization must develop a platform of things to be *for*." Diversity and a positive, proactive agenda for change were important for the early leaders of the organization and remain a focus for the State Governing Board today.

---

**LEADER SPOTLIGHT: ELIZABETH LA GRUA**

"One of the reasons I'm so glad to be a part of Virginia Organizing is that we are *doing* something—we take action," said Elizabeth La Grua of the Staunton/Augusta/Waynesboro Chapter. "There is a plan to make things better and I am a part of that as a local community leader."

*The Virginia Organizing Project's initial approach is reflected in an early grant proposal written to the Unitarian Universalist Veatch Program at Shelter Rock:*

Our overall method can be illustrated by the following analogy. A large rock is blocking an important highway. Twenty-five people are pushing as hard as they can on the rock, but it won't move. Someone finally says, "Why don't we figure out how many people we really need to move this rock?" Using all the skills in the group, a sound analysis is done and the group determines that 1,000 people are needed to move the rock. The 25 they have now could push and push and push, but they are never going to move that rock. So they stop pushing and figure out how they are going to recruit the 975 additional people they need. Then everyone does it. It may take some time, but when the 1,000 people are gathered together, and they understand why they are there, the rock can be moved quickly.

We are trying to determine the power that we need to realize substantive long-term changes in Virginia. The time that it took to do the initial analysis and planning has been time very well invested. All too often organizations rely on 25 activists who waste their time pushing on a rock that they cannot move. We are developing a model for people to act differently, thinking in terms of power and long-term institutional change.

If people join together and learn about power, political and economic change, and can learn from past history and from other groups, we will be far more effective than continuing the pattern of simply working on individual policy campaigns. Virginians will learn about connections between the problems they are confronting. They need to understand these connections and then learn the necessary skills of public life to be effective in dealing with these issues.

With VOP's approach, many people see the results of working across constituency and issue lines to create a new political force. We have been able to get a lot of people to rethink their organizing strategies – this continues to be a major accomplishment as groups think and plan about what methods can be effective in the current climate. This often means changing their organizational structure, their training programs, issue selection, and so forth.

## THE ORGANIZING COMMITTEE

From the more than 250 people with whom Szakos spoke, 10 emerged as leaders to form the original Organizing Committee for the Virginia Organizing Project. The Organizing Committee met on August 19, 1995, and made decisions that still affect Virginia Organizing in 2015. They decided to build a political force in the state composed of low- to moderate-income people, people of color, people who identify as LGBT, and others traditionally excluded from Virginia political life because they were ignored by and excluded from traditional power structures. Organizing Committee members knew that some successful multi-racial organizations find that defining issues non-racially works best for them. But in Virginia, obvious patterns of racism and classism that serve to separate African-Americans and other people of color from whites, and low-income people from those who have financial means, had been glossed over for so long that explicit discussions of racism and classism provided a breath of fresh air to community leaders around the state. With diversity, power structures, and race relations in mind, the Organizing Committee answered questions like, "What would you like to see the Virginia Organizing Project do?" and brainstormed ideas about skills they would need – individually and collectively – to be more effective. They agreed to be broad and aim for structural change, and put a lot of thought into how to communicate with their home communities and connect with existing groups.

The Organizing Committee began to develop a Virginia-specific community organizing model, and to do so, they determined that they needed to learn the basic nuts and bolts of community organizing, focus on diversity, do some political, social, and economic analysis, and research existing models used by other groups, both locally and in other states. They each agreed to work on fundraising and to find more people with whom to conduct one-to-one conversations. Then they set their next meeting. The Virginia Organizing Project was born!

Over the next several months, members of the Organizing Committee visited a variety of groups throughout the country and read books and materials on community organizing. They analyzed the structures and strategies that could be used to build a statewide organization that would bridge the barriers of race, gender, class, sexual orientation, occupation, geography, and ability, and then began to write an Organizing Plan, the main components of which still guide the organization's work today. These components – building organizational capacity, strategic communications, working in coalitions and alliances, participating in issue campaigns that make sense, increasing grass-roots fundraising, and strengthening leadership development – have kept Virginia Organizing focused on the long-term goals and celebrating victories in various forms along the way.

"I remember being very skeptical at first," said Jill Carson, an Organizing Committee member and one of the driving forces behind the first Chapter in Lee County. "Going to Minnesota to visit an organization using the relationship-building method of community organizing in a rural area was a fantastic opportunity for me to see it in action – and learn more about how we could do it in Virginia."

"Things were moving fast," Carson said. "I shared stories with other Organizing Committee members from other parts of the state and quickly learned that we shared similar issues, particularly as they related to race, in spite of the distance between us. We saw the connections and were beginning to understand how this idea of relationship building with people of diverse backgrounds could result in developing a power base on a local and statewide basis.

"We in Lee County found ourselves, very early in the process, having to put this to the test when we decided to challenge the jury selection process in the county. It worked! This approach allowed us to fill the Lee County Courthouse to capacity with folks from across the state and get some things changed – the start of many successes.

"While many, many commendable things have evolved with VOP/Virginia Organizing over the past 20 years," Carson reflected, " the basic foundation has never wavered."

**THE ORGANIZING MODEL**

The Virginia Organizing Project refined and implemented an organizing model that attracts ordinary people for the long haul through an intentional leadership process that develops democratic skills and builds a sense of ownership and community. The organization's approach uses an intentional method of building one-to-one relationships among people of diverse backgrounds (see Appendix B for more details on conducting one-to-one conversations), identifying issues of concern, providing training in research and leadership, and implementing strategies that break down traditional divisions while achieving concrete results. Community organizing at

Virginia Organizing emphasizes the need to address current problems and build long-term, diverse leadership across the state. The model has succeeded where previous organizing efforts in Virginia had not: Virginia Organizing has created a statewide, multi-issue, diverse, membership-driven organization with staying power.

Early VOP meetings were interactive and visionary. At one meeting, leaders spent intentional time in pairs to strengthen their own relationships. Leaders' feedback on the experience was that they had a lot in common in terms of why they had gotten involved; that conversations like these get easier the more you have them; that staying focused can be difficult so training for one-to-ones is important to ensure quality; and that reporting back about one-to-ones for group processing and analysis is key for effectiveness. Leaders also divided into groups to draw pictures of what they hoped the organization would look like in the year 2000. According to the summary of their October 7, 1995, meeting, "The drawings reflected an 'enlightened' and well-organized citizenry!"

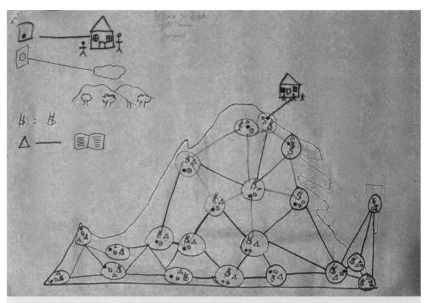

The original Organizing Committee wanted to connect people from all across the state to organize around common values. They realized that it is easy to be busy, but it is hard to be strategic. They invested the time necessary to develop solid – and strategic – plans.

The original Organizing Committee was dedicated to their vision. They created a job description for committee members, developed individual plans for things they wanted to learn, agreed to ask other people for donations, and did research tailored to their interests and skills. They also formed a subcommittee to begin drafting a mission statement and established a newsletter, first published in December 1995. The newsletter featured an introduction to VOP, a list of Organizing Committee members, a summary of the initial assessment based on one-to-one conversations, an article on legislative power and money, and a call for additions to the cardboard box library – a box of resources on community organizing, racism, and a wide range of social justice issues available for sharing with interested folks at various meetings.

## LEADER SPOTLIGHT: KATE ROSENFIELD

"The most meaningful part about working with Virginia Organizing is the input that volunteers have. In our Chapter meetings, everyone is given an opportunity to share what issues are important to them and what their thoughts are about the issues. At Chapter meetings, our organizer always involves new people in the discussions to gauge their interest on issues. What makes Virginia Organizing unique is the emphasis on using the skills and interests of volunteers to lead."

In March 1996, the Organizing Committee officially adopted the original mission statement:

*The Virginia Organizing Project (VOP) is a statewide grassroots organization dedicated to challenging injustice by empowering people in local communities to address issues that affect the quality of their lives. VOP especially encourages the participation by those who have traditionally had little or no voice in our society. By building relationships with individuals and groups throughout the state, VOP strives to get them to work together, democratically and non-violently, for change.*

A subcommittee drafted this statement based on key terms and ideas from all the Organizing Committee members, then members showed the draft to others in their communities to get some feedback, and after a few changes, it was officially adopted. Because of the intentional and deliberate wording developed by the Organizing Committee, the mission statement has remained virtually unchanged, except for the addition of the term "non-partisan" in 2013 to reinforce the nature of the work Virginia Organizing does as Virginia became a partisan battleground state for presidential elections and the state legislature became more polarized by party politics.

While the need for an organizing effort like VOP was long coming, it couldn't be built in a day. There was a lot to think through, and the Organizing Committee drafted policies and made strategic decisions that still affect Virginia Organizing today.

## RELATIONSHIPS REALLY DO MATTER

A central issue that many of the initial one-to-ones raised was racism. The group learned that this had also been a challenge in past attempts to create a statewide grassroots effort in Virginia – the effect of inequality and deeply ingrained racism was too strong for these organizations to survive. To counter this, VOP kept diversity at the forefront of all its efforts. Even further, VOP devoted substantial amounts of time and resources to Dismantling Racism workshops. Before the first VOP-initiated workshop, some Organizing Committee members attended a four-day session conducted by the Peace Development Fund and concluded: "We are convinced that developing a diverse organization is a challenge, but one that is more achievable if we are clear about our goals and expectations and put systems and structures in place that will enhance diversity." VOP members also learned through early training sessions that they needed to make the workshops as "Virginian" as possible (in terms of content, cultural context, and style) and more participatory than other models. They had to develop exercises that made sense to local community groups wanting to tackle race on personal, local, and statewide levels. Overall, the kind of diversity the founders wanted for VOP was not only multi-racial but also multi-constituency.

Many attempts at creating statewide organizations have centered around a linear approach, running specific progressive issue campaigns, and bringing together major existing players – unions, seniors, progressive legislators – to push for changes. Other statewide change efforts have centered on electoral politics.

As an organization seeking to do things a little differently, VOP was willing to experiment over the years with other approaches. VOP borrowed heavily from the models that use relationship building at their core, but differed in one major way: the organization looked outward to the community more than inward to the needs of the organization. Most other relationship-based models are highly controlled, with tight timelines and specific demands of specific targets. Their formula is simple – win, celebrate, and move on to the next issue campaign. While some include leadership development activities, few tackle systemic oppression in a deliberate way. VOP sought to do more than just issue or campaign organizing.

VOP set out to build a web of public relationships across a wide range of constituencies. This meant people had to learn how to interact with those much different than themselves. But VOP also decided to tackle racist institutions, discrimination based on sexual orientation, and unfair wages. While other statewide groups were taking a narrower approach to make changes to a particular policy, VOP was pushing for a broader agenda to change systems of oppression as well.

VOP looked – and still looks – at power as a fluid concept that can shift under the right conditions. Issue campaigns are vehicles that a lot of people can rally around, but can also be used as learning tools to build more power and leadership skills. VOP wanted more people to learn about power, to be able to recognize it, to be able to make changes that benefit all people, not just those in power!

VOP continuously looked for opportunities to bring the widest range of constituencies together to make a difference, no matter where that might be – locally, regionally, or statewide. The VOP Statement of Beliefs, which gives a positive direction to the grassroots organizing, and the Annual Organizing Plan, which provides specific direction in a given year, were always guiding the process strategically to bring harmony to the diversity of issues. With VOP's long-term goals in place, these elements contributed to a cohesive strategy.

If VOP provided an overall framework (multi-issue, multi-constituency, long-term change, moving people to action) and made sure that attention was given to all the elements of organizational development (power analysis, strategic thinking, continuous expansion, fundraising/resources, leadership development, political education), then the relationship building approach would be done in a way so that VOP leaders were agitating, nurturing, challenging, supporting, and promoting social change in a variety of ways that were enriching, rather than limiting. Diversity adds new ideas and perspectives that may help discover creative solutions to difficult problems, but most importantly, a focus on diversity is a commitment to honoring the worth of every person.

## DISMANTLING RACISM WORKSHOPS

The Dismantling Racism workshop provides an opportunity to explore concepts and theories focused on race and racism. Recruitment for workshops is intentional in order to get broad demographic representation and people who are committed to taking action. Facilitators provide a safe space for participants to discuss and learn about racism

Participants do a "crossover" exercise in a Dismantling Racism workshop in Richmond.

and figure out barriers to organizing together to make changes in local communities as well as statewide.

Using participatory exercises based on personal experiences, shared learning, and critical thinking about institutions in our society, the workshop provides a better understanding of internalized racist oppression and white privilege. It helps participants develop a common analysis of their experiences about personal, cultural, and institutional racism and how to work together for long-term social change. The workshop agenda includes a "Taking It Home" session, which gives participants time to work together in small groups and identify ways to put into action what they have learned in the workshop.

The workshop curriculum was refined by Virginia Organizing staff and volunteer facilitators after researching many other models and approaches and continues to be revisited and updated. The workshop (one day or three days) specifically uses examples of racism in Virginia to ground the learning in a state-specific context.

## FOUNDATIONAL CONCEPTS

The Virginia Organizing Project would have looked like some other organizations whose failure many Virginians had already witnessed if inclusivity and diversity were not prioritized in structural decisions about the organization. How did the Organizing Committee learn from other organizations? They focused on community building by intentionally getting to know each other, including others from their communities in decisions, and staying open to ideas different from theirs. These very deliberate decisions made the difference and are still part of the culture of Virginia Organizing. Maintaining diversity and equality among the State Governing Board, Chapter leaders, and staff still remains a priority.

Another step for the Organizing Committee was making decisions about the structure of VOP once they had foundational concepts like diversity at the forefront. Different geographical areas could organize and form "Chapters," they decided, and then other existing organizations could join VOP's work as "Affiliates." The Organizing Committee set forth criteria for accepting Chapters and Affiliates which included both rights and responsibilities of these entities, and accepted the first VOP Chapter petition from residents of Lee County, Virginia, in April 1996. They also determined that each Chapter should have two representatives and each Affiliate one representative on the Board, and that the number of Affiliate representatives should never outweigh those from Chapters. (This was later briefly suspended when Chapter formation took longer than initially expected). The Organizing Committee set target sites for more Chapters, predicting that the process in each place could take anywhere from four to six months. This estimate was not accurate; it ended up taking much longer to build VOP Chapters.

Then, in 1996, the Organizing Committee, with their vision for a more just Virginia and strong foundation, made a three-year Organizing Plan at their annual meeting in August. The Organizing Committee became the State Governing Board and created committees (Executive, Nominations, and Ad hoc planning committees for workshops and events) to govern various aspects of the organization. The plan also addressed organizational activities such as the annual power analysis (to take an honest look at who has power in Virginia), statewide campaigns, staffing, fundraising, media and communications, leadership development, and guidelines for relating to outside groups.

As these key decisions were being made and new Chapters were being formed via one-to-one meetings, specific activities emerged from the Affiliates, including a Workers' Memorial Day rally and an opportunity to take action on hate crimes legislation before the state legislature. These activities were part of broader campaigns to strengthen workers' rights and address racial injustice. The Lee County Chapter held a Dismantling Racism workshop, created working groups to investigate new areas for action, and continued the relationship building process via one-to-one meetings with community members. As a part of their efforts to address racism in their county, they helped establish a Council on Cultural Diversity that worked to inform public officials and other residents of issues of racism in the community and ways to work toward a better future. Community members reported, "We have been able to get our public officials and other residents to come to the Council on Cultural Diversity meetings to learn more about racism and prepare for the future," and, "The Council has raised further awareness and sensitivity regarding racism in the county."

A successful 1996 for VOP ended with a newsletter to supporters about the recent adoption of the Organizing Plan, leader awards, a job announcement for a community organizer, and an article by June Rostan, director of the Southern Empowerment Project. In her article on leadership development, "It's a Gift to be Simple—Lessons in Leadership," Rostan highlighted simple down-to-earth guidelines for recognizing good leaders and leadership development:

- Good leaders have followers.
- The most vocal people are not necessarily the best leaders.
- Good leaders share their knowledge, skills and teach others.
- Good leaders are team players.
- Good leaders know when they need to step aside.
- A good leader spends more time listening than talking.
- A good leader is not a "glory hog."
- The best leaders lead by example.
- The best leaders are able to identify with other people's experiences of oppression.
- The best leaders can dream and take risks.

Rostan also pointed out that the best leadership development is done in and with groups, ideally in organizations with goals designed to improve the community for everybody. Good leadership development holds leaders accountable, she wrote, and good leadership programs are effective regardless of the amount of formal education a person has. VOP took that message to heart and established a strong culture of leadership development.

After the initial Organizing Committee was established, VOP convened a meeting of seasoned community organizers from across the country to talk about VOP's initial organizing assessment of Virginia. This is an excerpt from an article by Joe Szakos and Ladelle McWhorter, "Virginia Organizing: The Action Is at the State Level," which was published in *Transforming Places: Lessons from Appalachia*, edited by Stephen L. Fisher and Barbara Ellen Smith, University of Illinois Press, 2012 (pages 186-187):

The...meeting consisted of experienced organizers who had been rethinking their approaches to community organizing since the Reagan years. Previously, the standard approach was to mount a series of issue campaigns. Organizers identified an issue people wanted to tackle by asking two questions: "What do you want, and who can give it to you?" Usually unstated was another question: "How will this campaign lead to the next and make our organization stronger?" Organizations were built one campaign at a time, growing bigger through each in preparation for the next. But by the 1990s, many organizers were thinking differently. Just getting local officials to pave a road, build more public housing, or stop a hazardous waste incinerator was not enough, even if each victory left their organizations better positioned to win the next campaign. Without *structural* change, they would face a succession of tough issue campaigns with no guarantee of long-term improvement in people's lives. Organizers began to seek lasting changes that could give communities more access and a stronger voice over the long haul. Hence, they added another question: "How does our present campaign push for long-term structural changes?

Of course, community organizing has always been about power; the main challenge is to achieve sufficient power—real and/or per-ceived—to get what the organization wants. Building power was the point of developing organizations through issue campaigns, and power took on even more importance when organizers prepared to work for structural change. But our meeting participants were not interested in just seeing Virginia Organizing moving power from one institutional site to another. They believed that to be broadly effective, organizing in Virginia would have to involve lots of people dealing with local as well as statewide problems and long-term, sustainable solutions involving fundamental structural change.

For that work, Virginia Organizing would need what Richard L. Wood calls "mobilizing capacity," the ability to turn out people for direct action or generate calls and letters to key political leadership on short notice. And more important, it would need to develop "strategic capacity," the ability to adapt to take advantage of changing circumstances – including opportunities not only for forging new relationships with political leaders but also involving new groups of people and incorporating new resources and technologies. Each organizational move, therefore, had to contribute to the systematic accumulation of political capacity.

Virginia Organizing thus began as an experiment in organizing dictated by geographical, political, and historical circumstances whose far-reaching implications only became clear to its founders as the organization took shape. The experiment was affected by the ways its organizers and members confronted the four challenges: expanding to scale, creating and maintaining broadly open organizational structures, preparing to adapt to changing circumstances, and ensuring that decision making is transparent and inclusive. Given historical contingencies in Virginia, these four challenges emerged as matters to be resolved among existing groups *and* as issues to be addressed within a single, extremely diverse, rapidly growing statewide organization. All four have had an impact, in both positive and negative ways, on our ability to build strategic capacity.

- We believe that all people should be treated fairly and with dignity in all aspects of life, regardless of race, class, gender, religion, sexual orientation, age, ability, or country of origin.
- We believe that every person in the Commonwealth is entitled to a living wage and benefit package that is sufficient to provide the basic necessities of life, including adequate housing, a nutritious diet, proper child care, sound mental and physical health care, and a secure retirement.
- We believe that every person is entitled to an equal educational opportunity.
- We believe that community, economic, social, and environmental policy should be developed with the greatest input from the people it is meant to serve, and that the policies should promote, celebrate and sustain the human and natural resources of Virginia.
- We believe in the elimination of the extremes of wealth and poverty, in a progressive tax system based on the ability to pay, and in making the nation's financial systems, including the Federal Reserve Bank, more responsive to the average citizen's needs.
- We believe that we should enhance and celebrate diversity in our community and in our state.
- We believe that those who have positions of authority in our governmental bodies, law enforcement agencies and institutions of learning should reflect the diversity of our communities.
- We believe that our public officials should be held accountable for their actions and decisions.
- We believe in the rights of workers, consumers, shareholders, and taxpayers to democratic self-organization.
- We believe in the elimination of the death penalty in all cases because it is fundamentally inhumane, ineffective as a deterrent to crime, and disproportionately and unjustly applied against people of color and those who are economically or educationally disadvantaged.
- We believe that physical and mental health are parts of personal and community well-being; we believe that Virginians have a broad public health and economic interest in ensuring that adequate care is available to low and moderate-income residents.

*The original was slightly modified; this is the current version as of October 2015.

# CHAPTER 2

# Strengthening the Foundation

**IN 1997, A SIGNIFICANT** portion of VOP activities included conducting workshops and getting out educational resources. Dismantling Racism workshops continued and VOP held trainings for people to become workshop facilitators to increase the capacity for the organization's reach and depth. Many other activities at the organizational level kept the Board active. The Board drafted and adopted a Statement of Beliefs, adopted a logo, began the VOP E-Action Alert System, began a program to collect and distribute used computers (for those who wished to participate in the action alert system) and supported Chapters and Affiliates.

VOP developed a Statement of Beliefs (see sidebar, left) when the opportunity was presented to sign onto a letter to Members of Congress from organizations in various states regarding policies of the Federal Reserve Bank.

The original logo of the Virginia Organizing Project focused on diversity, statewide scope, and continued growth of the organization.

The State Governing Board agreed that the letter aligned with what VOP stood for, but without an actual statement, that was a subjective decision. So, they embarked on a process of creating a Statement of Beliefs. First, all Board members wrote out statements they felt represented the organization. Then they met, chose the best statements, and hashed out the Statement of Beliefs to help guide their work and help them be strategic about the campaigns and actions the organization would tackle. Because of this early work, what VOP stands for is clear to anyone who reads the Statement of Beliefs or participates in a Chapter. The Statement of Beliefs helps to explain to a newcomer that the organization is about a lot of different things, that VOP values diversity, and that it is acceptable for everyone not to agree on everything.

The Wythe County Chapter was officially accepted as VOP's second Chapter in time for the Founding Convention in June 1997. At the convention, participants had one-to-one meetings to meet new people and build relationships, attended a variety of workshops, accepted Chapters and Affiliates, and held a cultural celebration with the Evangelistic Choraliers, Solfud and John McCutcheon.

## ANNUAL POWER ANALYSIS

Power analysis sessions are still held every year on the last weekend of April, involving Board members, key Chapter leaders, and staff who join together to figure out the power landscape in the Commonwealth.

Leaders shared a light moment at the 2014 Power Analysis.

## LAYING A SOLID FOUNDATION: POWER ANALYSIS AND GRASSROOTS FUNDRAISING

The Board also began their strategic planning for the future by considering what criteria should be in place to begin their first statewide issue campaign. They discussed who held power in the state and what they needed to do to shift the balance of power. This was the beginning of an annual power analysis to clarify the organization's strengths, weaknesses, as well as to identify potential allies and adversaries for its social change efforts.

## EVALUATION QUESTIONS FROM 1998

- Have we developed a model of organizing that draws from the strengths of other models, but does not have the same limitations?
- Have we figured out a way to have people develop groups faster and stronger and have more of these groups throughout the state?
- How does the one-to-one approach help or hinder organizational development and issue work?
- Have we been able to put materials in people's hands that will help them process the complications of an international economy in a way that they can take direct actions to make a difference?
- What new leadership skills are people learning as a part of VOP's work? What is missing?
- Have we helped people work through their own racism and sexism and other "isms" and work together to changed those societal structures that keep people from realizing their full potential?
- What is the effect of having a lot of Dismantling Racism workshops as part of our work?
- Does having a multi-racial constituency affect issue selection and organizational development of VOP?
- Have we helped people understand what power is, what it looks like, how it is used?
- As we deliberately work to build relationships with other organizations who are not Chapters or Affiliates, does that make VOP more effective? How?
- Are people now organized in ways that get them some of that power, that make their lives fuller and that make their communities better places in which to live?

As a result, VOP set a goal to develop good working relationships with key staff of the Virginia AFL-CIO, the Virginia NAACP, and the Virginia Council of Churches, among others.

The first annual fall fundraising campaign also began in 1997. Grassroots fundraising is critical to continuing important community organizing work because it provides money for the organization to pursue its goals. Overall, Virginia Organizing's fundraising strategy began, and has remained, multi-faceted over the years. For instance, early on, VOP systematically solicited individual donations and Chapters and Affiliates paid dues. The organization also started a pledge system for donors who agreed to pay a certain amount over time. VOP also held grassroots events (dessert parties, raffles, benefit concerts, etc.) to help expand the donor base, and established a sliding-scale fee system for workshop registrations; ads were sold to organizations and businesses for the annual meeting program book; and Virginia Organizing continued to apply for grants from new sources. Because a lot of groups get funding from government grants, and then risk losing their funding if they question any actions of the government, VOP leaders decided early on to avoid government grants and to raise necessary funds for the work in other ways.

## ANNUAL EVALUATION BEGINS

Based on the power analysis and the Organizing Plan, a thorough evaluation is conducted by the State Governing Board in November each year, a process that began in 1998 (see sidebar on previous page). They ask the question: Have we changed the balance of power in Virginia? The answer in the early years was typically, "No, but we are on the right track." Other questions helped the Board identify what activities had been done, what worked and what didn't, and how to structure the next year's Organizing Plan.

## CHAPTERS AND AFFILIATES

As the State Governing Board moved forward in 1998, they planned strategically to continue to shift the balance of power in Virginia by paying attention to current trends affecting power relationships and involving the voices of directly affected people who have traditionally been left out and rendered powerless. In an effort to stay multi-issue, one idea was to tackle a package of issues in conjunction with various groups in the state. This was VOP's way of saying that "in the same way that we think that if individuals can come together and work together they'll be more powerful, we think that if groups come together and work together, we'll all be more powerful."

The way the Board implemented this was through the Affiliate model, a practice of VOP that continued until 2004. After five years of experimentation, the Board concluded that just because groups sign on to a common agenda does not mean that they are willing to increase their organizing capacity to run successful campaigns, and groups were reluctant to put time and energy into campaigns that were not directly related to their own issue agendas.

Virginia Forest Watch, a VOP affiliate, gathered to challenge clear cutting and bad logging practices in Dickenson County.

Theoretically, they bought into "borrowing and sharing power" but some were more interested in the "borrowing" part of the equation. In 2004, VOP dropped Affiliates from the organizational structure and concentrated on getting more Chapters, those local units that were 100 percent behind VOP's philosophy and "deep" organizing approach.

### BUILDING AN IDENTITY

Another early task of the Board was developing a recognizable identity as an organization. In one meeting VOP Board members were divided into groups and asked to come up with a "bumpersticker slogan" to frame the VOP message. Early options included:
- Voice of the people
- A new approach to old problems
- The people's voice is the people's choice
- No one is expendable
- Turn up the volume, organize!
- Power = quality of life
- Vision of the people – views of the people
- Grassroots power for long-term change

## LAYING DOWN EVEN DEEPER ROOTS

VOP continued to grow, and in late 1998, purchased a modest office building in Charlottesville to have a permanent home. Leaders felt so good that VOP was here to stay! During the next year, in addition to the director (Szakos), VOP staff totaled four organizers, an administrative director, and a development director. A great portion of the work for these staff involved organizing new Chapters that were diverse, multi-issue, organizing locally, and working for long-term change; consulting with other groups; and holding workshops. Around this time, VOP focused on the campaigns that addressed racism, heterosexism, living wage, and public housing initiatives. These campaigns were part of broader long-term issues that VOP had selected to work on, including anti-discrimination and economic justice. Staff and leaders trained to become facilitators of Dismantling Racism workshops and developed a curriculum for Exploring Heterosexism workshops. Fighting the "isms" was very important to the early Boards of VOP. They saw these oppressive aspects of Virginia culture as barriers preventing change.

Staff helped leaders in the local Chapters and other groups learn about community organizing strategies and grassroots fundraising in an attempt to expand the work and connect single-issue groups to the greater vision for the multi-issue, multi-constituency political force that VOP was aiming to become.

VOP published a 32-page quarterly magazine starting in 1998, *virginia.organizing.* The publication presented articles on issues based on the work of VOP Chapters and Affiliates, gave news of other groups in

Wythe County VOP Chapter leaders met with officials of the Federal Reserve Bank of Richmond, and convinced the Richmond Fed Vice President to set up the first rural economic workshop to study the needs of rural counties.

the state, as well as "Organizing Toolbox" articles (in English and Spanish) like "Win and Build the Power of Your Organization" and "Elements of Strategy: Constituents, Allies and Opponents" and "Tips for Chairing Meetings." It eventually had a circulation of 6,500, connecting readers to the organizing work going on in Virginia in a unique way.

An excerpt from a chapter by Michael Dennis, "Democratic Vistas in the Old Dominion: Organizing for Change among Working Virginians," in his book, *The New Economy and the Modern South,* University Press of Florida, 2009 (p. 241):

> Instead of generating support for policies that favored tax breaks for stock investors, atrophic monetary practices, and federal debt repayment that undermined social programs, the VOP set out to restore the idea that government action in the economic sphere could benefit average southerners.
>
> It did so by challenging the assumption that the economic rules governing American life were fixed, inflexible, and resistant to modification. The VOP brought into question the motives of policy elites and the interests served by the highest levels of economic power. By informing participants "about major trends – from the surge in income inequality to the growing power of financial investors over a broad range of economic decisions," the VOP questioned the basic axioms of American economic life in the late twentieth century.

A key section in *virginia.organizing* was "Understanding the Economy," a part of a larger VOP movement toward popular education surrounding the economy. VOP began working with the Federal Reserve Bank of Richmond, encouraging them to involve low-income and working class people in how they conducted their work. VOP hosted four tours for the "Fed." First, Federal Reserve Bank of Richmond President J. Alfred Broaddus, Jr. toured Martinsville with VOP to meet with low-wage manufacturing plant workers, particularly injured workers, and then northern Virginia communities to learn about affordable housing issues there. VOP members then took him to visit the Eastern Shore to learn about community development and economic development plans in that region. Later, several officials of the Federal Reserve Bank of Richmond toured Louisa County in order to inform the Community Development Advisory Council about projects that could be beneficial. The Community Development Advisory Council had been formed in 1998 in response to the call by many groups, organized by Tom Schlesinger of the non-profit Financial Markets Center, urging President Broaddus to have a specific mechanism to hear the interests of small businesses, labor, and community development groups.

Community leaders got the Federal Reserve Bank of Richmond to convene local bankers on the Eastern Shore to provide financing to struggling African-American communities there and to undertake in Wythe County its first economic development study of a rural Virginia community. VOP got the Richmond "Fed" to focus thought and energy on helping to figure out more grassroots solutions to large economic problems, something federal agencies were not routinely doing.

VOP leaders stand together in Accomack County on the Eastern Shore, one of the many locations where they met in the early years. Their visionary leadership utilized diverse ideas to create an organization unlike anything in Virginia.

Other efforts concerning the economy included living wage campaigns. In 1998, there was a successful campaign in Alexandria, Virginia, which sparked VOP to begin or support similar campaigns in Charlottesville, at the University of Virginia, and then in Albemarle County. VOP was eventually involved in more than a dozen living wage campaigns in various localities and on six college campuses. VOP also tried living wage campaigns aimed at low-wage private employers, and targeted Courtyard by Marriott in Charlottesville: protests outside Courtyard by Marriott occurred every Friday for 107 straight weeks, resulting in the Mayor of Charlottesville working with local hotel operators and Piedmont Virginia Community College to link job training with increased wages.

In other areas, VOP helped an Affiliate, the Montebello Clean Mountain Coalition, to get the Central Virginia Electric Cooperative to honor landowner requests to refrain from spraying pesticides under power lines on private property, and to maintain vegetation manually. Working with other groups, the Montebello Clean Mountain Coalition also got 10,000 acres in Nelson County designated as federal wilderness area. VOP was able to generate phone calls from people all across the state to support both of these campaigns—examples of how a statewide grassroots base could provide important support for local and regional issues.

Led by four student interns in 1999-2000, VOP succeeded in a campaign to convince the Charlottesville School Board to add sexual orientation to the non-discrimination policy for students and employees. VOP also successfully challenged the Alexandria Housing and Redevelopment Authority to issue notices in both English and Spanish because of the changing demographics of the residents. New Chapters were formed in Lynchburg and Wise County and leadership trainings were held across the state; prior to VOP, there were few options for local grassroots organizations to find leadership training and consulting on organizational development concerns.

## THE FIRST LOCAL VICTORY

In late 1998, VOP celebrated the first major local victory! The VOP Chapter in Lee County successfully challenged the jury selection process used in the county at the time as not fair to people of color. As a result of the campaign, a new jury selection system was implemented, and for the first time ever, an African-American served as a jury commissioner. The county changed the selection process for the jury "pool" by moving to a random selection process instead of the previous system in which five white men chose their friends for the jury pool, effectively eliminating people of color and low-income residents.

## BUILDING ORGANIZATIONAL CAPACITY

After five years, the original Organizing Committee had created an organization that was on track to become a strong grassroots political force. They had strategically chosen not to take on their own statewide campaign in those early years as they focused on building local power at the Chapter level and supporting Affiliates. Simultaneously, they developed other aspects of organizational capacity and focused on statewide economic education activities.

VOP leaders were learning many lessons about how to organize to change Virginia. Practical experience helped people see the bigger picture in a way that just talking about it does not. Over time, this method developed a seasoned group of leaders and an expectation that the organization would continue pulling in new people to define new issues and take action on them, thus becoming leaders themselves.

VOP organized to integrate theory and practice and make connections between local problems and larger structures and events. VOP challenged people to move beyond the parochialism that often characterizes political and intellectual life in the United States. Confronting power and privilege in workshops and through direct action was not and is not easy, but it is necessary to empower individuals to change their lives and communities for the better.

A solid foundation for the organization was laid. What made VOP so effective was a particular kind of integrity, a strong sense of the difference between right and wrong that moves people to action. Early on, it was important to the organization to do what they said they were going to do and not overcommit and underdeliver. This commitment framed VOP as realistic and leaders knew they could trust the organization. VOP saw, and continues to see, the worries of ordinary people as legitimate and central and is able to link these cares and worries to broader issues of public life.

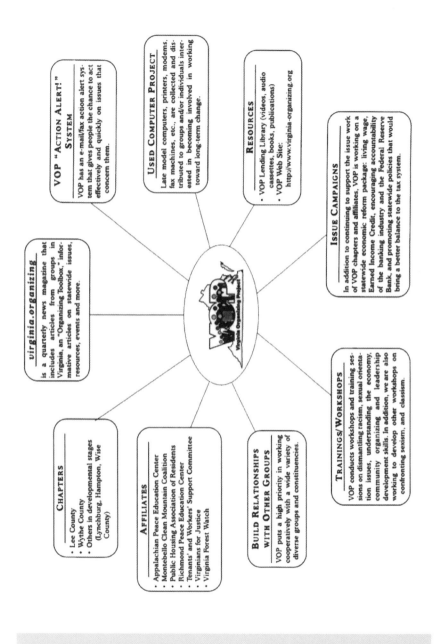

This was a handout used in 1999 to explain the Virginia Organizing Project.

There are many versions of this story; this one is adapted from "The Parable of Good Works" by Richard Gilbert, which appeared in *The Prophetic Imperative: Social Gospel in Theory and Practice*, published by Skinner House Books in 2000. VOP leaders and staff often use this story to explain how the organization is working for structural change:

> Once upon a time there was a small village on the edge of a river. The people there were good and life in the village was good. One day a villager noticed a baby floating down the river. The villager quickly swam out to save the baby from drowning. The next day this same villager noticed two babies in the river. She called for help, and both babies were rescued from the swift waters. And the following day four babies were seen caught in the turbulent current. And then eight, then more, and still more!
>
> The villagers organized themselves quickly, setting up watchtowers and recruiting swimmers who could resist the swift waters and rescue babies. They held special trainings and rescue squads were soon working 24 hours a day. And each day the number of helpless babies floating down the river increased. The villagers organized themselves efficiently. The rescue squads were now snatching many children each day. While not all the babies, now very numerous, could be saved, the villagers felt they were doing well to save as many as they could each day. Indeed, the village priest blessed them in their good work. And life in the village continued on that basis.
>
> One day, however, someone raised the question, "But where are all these babies coming from? Let's organize a team to head upstream to find out how these babies are getting into the river in the first place!"

# CHAPTER 3

# The First Statewide Campaign: Affordable Housing

**DURING ITS INITIAL PLANNING**, the founding Organizing Committee had made a decision that VOP would not undertake any signature statewide campaigns for the first five years so that a solid grassroots base of support could be built. In 2000, after five years of building relationships and Chapters and learning new skills, the State Governing Board was ready to plan for a new direction. A subcommittee of the Board conducted a power analysis at their December retreat and agreed to pursue affordable housing as the first statewide campaign from a variety of options.

"The shortage of affordable housing is a common denominator in local communities all over Virginia," wrote Andy Kegley in a reflection about VOP's first statewide campaign. Even though VOP had been supporting local and even some state-level campaigns of Chapters and Affiliates since the beginning, 2001 marked the first official VOP statewide campaign.

| |
|---|
| develop major campaign in 2001 |
| add more staff |
| expand infrastructure (database, action alerts, used computer equipment, etc.) |
| expand media exposure |
| raise more money (grants and grassroots) |
| expand leader trainings |
| expand organizer trainings |
| build stronger relationships with other groups |
| add interns |
| complete clearer power analysis |
| field staff gets more experienced |
| existing chapters/affiliates get stronger |
| add more chapters/affiliates |
| continue building relationships |
| continue/expand existing trainings (racism, sexual orientation, economy, leadership skills) |

A handout like the one above was used by the State Governing Board to look at all the building blocks for the growing organization (2000-2001).

In 2000, Virginia was number one in the United States in unaffordable rental housing according to a study done by the National Low-Income Housing Coalition. Thirty-four percent of renters in Virginia could not afford to rent a two-bedroom apartment at market rates; a minimum wage worker had to work 94 hours a week in order to afford a two-bedroom apartment, according to the study.

VOP research indicated that the Virginia Housing and Development Authority (VHDA) had a major fund balance surplus, a portion of which could be used to finance low- and moderate-income rental housing and home mortgages. Because leaders and staff had talked to people from a wide variety of constituencies, VOP Board members expressed an interest in including other VHDA policy issues in the campaign: loans to unrelated couples (same-sex couples and domestic partners), loans for cooperative housing, and eliminating the question of immigrant status in obtaining a loan. They were also concerned that interest rates were too high and the down payments that VHDA wanted were out of reach of those who really needed affordable housing.

## SETTING GOALS FOR THE CAMPAIGN

To pursue affordable housing access for more Virginians, the State Governing Board adopted seven goals for the campaign:
1. winning the issue – getting more affordable housing units;
2. developing/strengthening local community groups;
3. involving people who have never been involved before, including youth;
4. developing a strong political education component of the campaign;
5. organizing local or regional committees for the campaign;
6. framing the issue in a way that relates to the power dynamics in the state; and,
7. creating a core group of at least 10 spokespeople in different parts of the state.

The State Governing Board established a statewide Affordable Housing Strategy Committee which identified possible endorsers, reviewed research on VHDA board members, and discussed a report by the Joint Legislative Audit and Review Commission (JLARC) of the Virginia General Assembly. The JLARC reported that:

*"VHDA has financial strength that should result in increased allocations to the Virginia Housing Fund, a fund that provides loans to house low- and very low-income persons, VHDA needs to do more to meet its public*

*mission and should be more accountable to the General Assembly, VHDA has not utilized some federal funds allocated to Virginia for the Section 8 program, and several aspects of the Section 8 program have not been adequately managed, and multi-family housing financed by VHDA is not affordable to the majority of tenants, and the approval process for the allocation of financing for multi-family properties could better address the housing needs of different regions of the State."*

(Staff Briefing, http://jlarc.virginia.gov/meetings/June00/VHDAbrief.pdf, found at http://jlarc.virginia.gov/reports.shtml)

The housing finance programs administered by the VHDA were funded by federal tax dollars, federal tax credits, and public tax-exempt and taxable bonds. It was clear that public funds were not being used as effectively as was possible and were not being used for their intended purpose. VOP saw this as an opportunity to help shape some important policy decisions that could drastically change the lives of real people.

By the middle of 2001, the VOP Affordable Housing Strategy Committee had framed the issue this way:

*VHDA has been under fire for its gross lack of attention to its public mission, and is likely to continue to be. However, unlike North Carolina, for example, Virginia does not have an effective statewide housing reform coalition. VOP will play an important role in attempting to redirect VHDA funds into affordable housing around the state, build-ing on six years of promoting a multi-issue agenda. Put simply, we will bring together groups whose main focus is racism, gay rights, environ-mental concerns, education, etc., but who we are now able to help make broader connections of systematic problems – they are now committed to a multi-issue statewide agenda. Building a strategic alliance on affordable housing should lead to work on other statewide policy issues in the future, too.*

The VHDA issue was about power and marginalization. VHDA was con-trolled by a 10-member board appointed by the Governor. Some of these members had personal financial interests in for-profit housing and others were either major campaign contributors to the Governor or family mem-bers of high-level politicians. Just as VOP was committed to having a diverse and representative board, so was their expectation of the board of VHDA.

## EIGHT PROPOSED VHDA CHANGES

1. Redirect home-ownership loans toward borrowers unable to afford private mortgages and use VHDA's financial strength to substantially reduce mortgage interest rates for low-income borrowers.
2. End discrimination against unrelated adults and documented immigrants otherwise eligible for VHDA financing.
3. Direct multi-family housing financing toward new construction and rehabilitation of existing units that rent at more than 30 percent of income for renters and 30-50 percent of median income.
4. Reduce displacement of residents due to VHDA-financed projects that result in substantial rent increases.
5. Encourage long-term retention of affordable housing units through the financing of cooperative, non-profit housing developments, and other creative approaches that reduce the loss of affordable units to market-rate rents after VHDA financing is repaid.
6. Provide consistent and timely administration of the Section 8 program, including uniform inspection procedures and fair reimbursement of administrative costs to local agencies that administer VHDA Section 8 programs.
7. Immediately redirect at least $600 million of VHDA's surplus toward low-interest financing, gap financing, equity investments, and other creative financing solutions that serve Virginians at 30-50 percent of median income, keep housing costs within 30 percent of household income for low-income borrowers and renters, and serve the special needs of elderly, disabled, and homeless Virginians.
8. Encourage the governor to appoint VHDA Board members representative of the nine housing-market regions of the state, low-income borrowers, non-profit housing developers, and private organizations that serve Virginians with the most critical housing needs, including the elderly, the disabled, and the homeless.

VOP wanted VHDA to be more accountable to the needs of Virginians, and sent eight proposed changes to the VHDA leadership. VOP also attended public meetings and requested individual meetings with commissioners. VOP leaders and staff met with more than 170 faith communities, agencies, and organizations to explain the affordable housing campaign and ask for their participation. Additionally, VOP began reporting on the VHDA's practices in *virginia.organizing*, encouraging the following actions: write letters to the editors of local newspapers about VHDA's surplus funds and the need for more affordable housing options in Virginia; ask for endorsements of VOP's work from faith communities and civic and professional groups; ask county boards of supervisors, city councils and local housing development agencies to endorse VOP's efforts; go to VHDA meetings if they lived near Richmond; and, write letters directly to members of the VHDA Board of Commissioners.

## GETTING RESULTS

The first win came in mid-2001 when VHDA allowed documented immigrants to have access to VHDA's loans. Eventually, VHDA added a public comment period before meetings. They even moved the meetings to a larger venue to have room for public attendance at meetings. Andy Kegley noted, "I remember the first time some members of the VOP committee and staff attended a VHDA Board meeting and had to sit on the windowsills in the board room because there was no seating provided for the public. Gradually, because we kept going back, the board meetings were held in larger rooms to accommodate the public."

These may seem like small victories, but they proved that the action alerts and the presence of VOP members at meetings were making a difference. VOP's next action alert encouraged constituents to contact the candidates then running for governor to ask them about their stance on the VHDA and how they planned to decide whom to appoint as members to the VHDA Board in the future.

By September 2001, VHDA had announced a new program, called SPARC (Sponsoring Partnerships and Revitalizing Communities), which would use $45 million in public tax-exempt bonds to provide homeownership loans at 5.5 percent interest for people who do not qualify for other VHDA loans. This was important because it had been found that nearly 40 percent of existing VHDA loan recipients could have afforded private loans and because this was a decreased interest rate from the normal 6.8 percent. There was a catch, of course: these loans would be offered in partnership with developers, non-profits, and local government groups and would therefore not be available statewide, and borrowers would have a limited selection of homes for which these loans would be available. Another announcement VHDA made was that they had voted to add a new member to the board, someone who is a Housing Choice Voucher Program (known as Section 8) recipient. Section 8 provides qualified low-income people with vouchers that can be used as partial payment of rent on privately-owned apartments selected by the voucher-holder. Adding this seat to the board was a small step toward increased diversity and an important way to ensure that directly affected people's experiences were being considered.

## LEADER SPOTLIGHT: ANDY KEGLEY'S STORY

A highlight for me was the trip through the snow to a VHDA public hearing in Richmond on changing its family rule, which prevents people unrelated by blood or marriage from pooling their resources to qualify for a VHDA loan. VOP Wythe County Chapter member Holly Farris and I left early in the morning to meet other folks in Charlottesville and then drive on to Richmond for the hearing. It had started to snow, which made driving pretty difficult, and just before we got to our exit on the Interstate in Richmond, the car broke down in a cloud of white smoke. We didn't know what had happened to the car at the time, but it turns out an axle broke. We all got out in the snow and scrambled to push it off the travel lane on the Interstate. Then a man stopped and asked if he could help us, and I asked him if he'd give us a ride to the VHDA. He agreed, and we jumped into his van, leaving one person with the car waiting for help. The hearing was about to start when we got there and since state offices had not yet closed due to the storm, the VHDA Board and staff decided to go ahead with the hearing. Lots of people spoke in favor of changing the rule, a few spoke against it. I really give credit to VHDA for going ahead with the hearing in spite of pressure from the opponents of changing the family rule to cancel it.

Andy Kegley is pictured (far left) with other members of the Virginia Organizing State Governing Board and staff (in front of the Charlottesville office).

Finally, the cover story of *virginia.organizing*'s first issue of 2002 provided even more good news: "Citizen persistence shapes VHDA decision: $283 million designated for low-income housing over five years!" The five-year plan financed low-income homeownership and rental housing construction loans at a 150 percent increase over previous years, and an additional $73 million was included for later in the five-year plan. An additional provision of the plan was for a three-member "creative financing team" to work with local governments, non-profits and developers to find new strategies for the low-income constituency.

VOP State Governing Board Chairperson Danielle Poux said, "This major change in priorities at VHDA demonstrates that ordinary people can have an effective voice in shaping major public policy decisions."

Andy Kegley's reflection also revealed that VHDA "financed a homeless shelter in Richmond recently. Think about that. In the past, housing advocates probably wouldn't even approach VHDA with anything unusual."

The fight for affordable housing in Virginia did not end with this win. Strategy is important, and here the story goes back to the local level. There was still misinformation and fear in local communities about affordable housing, even though low- and moderate-income rental units were badly needed and properly planned construction would improve the local tax base. Property owners were fearful of their own property values declining – a belief rooted in housing policies of the past that perpetuated racism and classism and clustered people of color and people with low incomes in specific neighborhoods. VOP members had to take the message to their locally elected city and county officials that affordable housing was a benefit to communities to make sure localities were able to take advantage of the new flow of funds for affordable housing. It was another important lesson VOP learned – an issue campaign does not always simply end with a policy change: it is important to have local leaders holding city and county officials accountable for follow through on those changes. This lesson would be utilized again years later when voting laws changed for the worse and Virginia Organizing was there to help ensure that local registrars were at least following these laws in a consistent and fair way.

Virginia Organizing has a strong commitment to provide opportunities for young people to learn about community organizing and social justice. Many young people are active members of our Chapters. In addition, from 1997-2014, we worked with 510 interns, with internships ranging from a few months to two years. Some received academic credit, some were paid, and the vast majority were Virginians.

Many interns show up at Virginia Organizing knowing that they want to do something to help make the world a more just place, but without all the practical skills to know how to make that happen. Interns often find their way to Virginia Organizing after being frustrated by classroom experiences that offer a history of poverty or injustice without an outlet for making change. And a lot of interns want to know that they aren't alone, that the radical notion

Virginia Organizing interns Noelle Garcia and Zach Hanson helped organize a Richmond Immigration Reform Rally. Interns have been an important part of Virginia Organizing's work for years.

of a small group of thoughtful, committed people changing the world isn't just a slogan for a bumper sticker.

Virginia Organizing's internships are all about learning: rather than assigning an intern a series of rote tasks, all internships begin with a conversation about what the intern wants to learn. Even when a new intern isn't sure how to articulate exactly what that learning might be, the message is clear: interning with Virginia Organizing is about building power for the organization as well as about developing the skills of interns.

The list of skills interns develop, and experiences interns have, is a lengthy one: interns participate in constituent meetings with elected officials, talk to people door-to-door about the changes they want to see in their neighborhood, learn to make coffee for community meetings, practice driving a stick shift in many a Charlottesville parking lot, and most importantly, interns learn that organizing work requires a delicate blend of patience and passion, and that being good to those around us helps us do even better work.

Internships at Virginia Organizing have often led to interns becoming organizers on their campuses, with Virginia Organizing, on political campaigns, and with community organizations across the country. Just as often, interns have gone on to work as guidance counselors, as social workers, as teachers and as a host of other professions where they continue to use skills they learn – facilitating a meeting, for instance, or writing a letter to the editor – to organize for change in their workplaces and communities.

For Virginia Organizing's part, internships are about intentionally recruiting young people, particularly women, people of color, and LGBTQ interns, to community organizing and social justice work, developing and training the next generations of change-makers (and learning from their experiences along the way!).

– Kevin Simowitz

# CHAPTER 4

# Organizing in More Communities

**VOP REMAINED STRATEGIC ABOUT** doing power analyses and constantly evaluating plans, campaigns, and programs. The State Governing Board, especially, took the broad "30,000 feet view" of Virginia – and of building the strategic organizing capacity of the organization – to see how the attempts to shift the balance of power, or "move the rock," were going. Besides setting benchmarks for issue campaigns, the Board also set annual goals for organizational capacity development: metrics for new members, number of people learning a new skill, number of people applying a skill, direct actions, meetings with public officials, phone banking calls, community forums and workshops, as well as increased visibility in the media. Because of constant analysis and evaluation of the strategic work, VOP was not afraid to make the changes necessary to keep the organization moving forward and to abandon ideas that no longer worked.

In 2004, it was clear that the Chapter-Affiliate model, while it had its strengths and had worked well to organize many groups, was not the most efficient for handling the statewide campaigns that VOP had started to pursue. The Board established a new model that removed Affiliates and redefined Chapters so they would have more depth. The new model also called for a much smaller, more strategic State Governing Board since at that point, Board membership numbers were in the twenties, consisting of Chapter leaders and Affiliate representatives, and were not very consistent. Additionally, the Board created strategy teams for statewide campaigns on criminal justice and tax reform, in addition to affordable housing. The statewide strategy committees allowed more people to participate in VOP's overall governance.

There were multiple reasons for these strategic changes. There were certain statewide campaigns that would be more effective to pursue legislatively, and this model created more potential power to affect change at that level. It also left room for local campaigns and showed the Virginia legislators that people were not only committed to speaking out on issues that were important to them as they met in Richmond once a year, but also that they had a presence in the local community and were committed to making change there, too. This all aligned with VOP's original commitments to being multi-issue and multi-constituency, involving the voices of directly affected and historically marginalized people, and remaining local and relevant to communities.

Chapters had specific roles: organizing local campaigns that made sense to their area; recruiting new members, especially those who were directly affected by the issues under consideration; maintaining e-mail and phone lists to be used for action alerts; fundraising; getting people to write op-eds and letters to the editor; recruiting for meetings with legislators before and after legislative sessions; and partnering with elected officials for policy development year round. The idea was that these organizing units – Chapters – of at least 25 diverse people could be called upon for action at the statewide level by other Chapters or in coalition with other organizations, and that they would be effective because of their strategic location with regards to elected officials with simultaneous vested interest in their locality. They would also be tied into ongoing VOP work like attending annual meetings, holding and participating in workshops, and sharing a broader long-term vision of social justice.

This shift also allowed for a role for active members who lived in areas without Chapters. They could be part of broader campaigns, calling or writing decision-makers, and putting pressure on their own legislators in the own districts. Eventually, VOP had members in every state legislative district – meaning that the organization could have constituent contact with every legislator. People who worked on statewide campaigns were encouraged to start a Chapter in their area, too.

The State Governing Board shift was also a major change. A nominating committee appointed by the Board was charged with paring the Board down to about 10 members once the Affiliates were removed. This was done with the idea that Board members selected would typically be more in tune with VOP's work and there would not be as much of a learning curve as when new people were constantly joining the Board. The reconstituted Board would therefore be better at evaluating VOP's efforts to make change at the statewide level, while also being representative of the local Chapters and therefore able to provide support to them. The revamped Board led to a more strategic and efficient use of time, energy, and resources.

It is important to note that VOP remained committed to continuing programs like Dismantling Racism workshops and sexual orientation workshops. The strategic commitment to raising consciousness of privilege, power, and the "isms" and how they affect social justice and marginalized people in Virginia remained a priority. Another key factor in the ongoing effectiveness of this new structure was the ongoing VOP priority of leadership development. Relating back to VOP's main concern for raising the voices of directly affected people, this commitment meant empowering individuals to make real change at a very grassroots level.

## DISMANTLING RACISM AND SOCIAL CHANGE

*Growing up in the United States, we have absorbed considerable misinformation, specifically negative information about people who are "different" than us and our families. We have been imprinted with negative beliefs, prejudices, and stereotypes about groups of people we barely know. This began to happen when we were young, when we couldn't distinguish truth from stereotype, before we could recognize misinformation or object. Now that we are older, we have a responsibility to think for ourselves.*

Thinking about the history of racism in the United States and how it continues to influence our structural systems is important to working for social change. Our assumptions based on this history, like the one above, are reviewed at every workshop. Recognizing that each of us makes decisions that affect others, Virginia Organizing encourages members to open themselves to a wider worldview.

Leadership development looks different for different people, but it hinges upon an individual's willingness to grow and their interest in creating change within the context of the VOP model and vision. For many leaders, this means getting involved because of one issue, such as affordable housing, but coming to understand the connection to other issues and the idea of "borrowing and sharing power" for these other things. In addition, thousands of people learned more about how power works in their communities. The organizing staff and leaders are still constantly doing one-to-one conversations in various communities throughout the state. These conversations center on what needs to be changed in a community, and inevitably, include discussions of power dynamics. In addition, Chapter meetings often include some leadership development training component, but leadership training programs were held separately from Chapter meetings as well.

## LEADERSHIP TRAINING

Participants in VOP leadership training have described the program as innovative, redefining leadership, nonformula, and not a textbook class. Participants shared the following statements:

*This is a work in progress – hands-on learning, not textbook learning.*
*The program is refreshing and a meaningful experience.*
*This is not just a "resume" builder.*
*I have increased my understanding and think more out of the box.*
*It's given us a better understanding of VOP as an organization, its history and the operating and organizing style.*
*We just don't learn in a vacuum because we immediately apply these new skills.*

## JOINT PLANS OF WORK

As a part of the effort to be multi-issue and multi-constituency from the very beginning, VOP helped other groups in varying ways over the years, especially small emergent groups aimed at structural change. As early as 2000, VOP began accepting grants and donations under its 501(c)(3) tax-exempt umbrella for these types of groups. There were a lot of benefits to this, including building more political power through interacting with more groups of people and creating goodwill toward VOP to balance the public's view of the organization as only focused on direct action. There were benefits for the groups as well, including getting group health insurance even if they only had one employee (because they became an employee of VOP), being able to offer tax deductions to donors, and not having to handle the administrative and financial tasks so they could stay focused on their core missions. The program gained popularity once word got out that VOP could provide these services, and some larger organizations were added as well.

By 2006, after the Affiliate model had been dropped and as VOP's own budget began to grow, it became necessary to redefine the ways VOP worked with other groups. VOP set up program accounts and labeled the groups in these programs as "Joint Plans of Work." The Board set parameters about the types of groups they would accept and about how they were incorporated into the organization through four program areas: Community Support, Environment, Transportation, and Human Rights. Over the years, the number of Joint Plans of Work programs has fluctuated between 20 and 40 and requests for Joint Plans of Work are still frequent. An inspiring amount of social justice and environmental work has been leveraged. Examples include a variety of youth development programs, a Catholic Worker community, a community bicycle program, an immigration coalition, anti-death penalty work, a computer recycling program, environmental work including a fossil-fuel-free farm, mountaintop and forest protection, green chemistry, urban agriculture and environmental nursing. One of the largest is Environmental Health Services, whose internationally known work connects science and the media on environmental health impacts and climate change.

Kara West, Operations Supervisor with Environmental Health Sciences (second from the right) reviews documents with Virginia Organizing's key administrative staff (from left) Sally Bastian, Laura Ramirez, and Michele Mattioli, who manage fundraising, accounting, administrative responsibilities, Joint Plans of Work, and other special projects.

"Virginia Organizing's 'Joint Plan of Work' program has been a godsend for Environmental Health Sciences," said CEO and Chief Scientist Pete Myers. "We've been part of Virginia Organizing since 2002. Over these dozen plus years, Virginia Organizing has been an extraordinarily and reliably efficient 'back office,' allowing us to focus on our substantive work. As a result, we've won national journalism awards, we've changed the public debate about toxic chemicals, and we've made real strides in enhancing people's health by alerting them to the need to reduce toxic exposures."

This Joint Plan of Work model still exists and continues to provide Virginia Organizing with a way to interact with communities in unique ways and build power with a wider constituency base for long-term social change. Virginia Organizing is selective about the groups with which it partners. Through a small administrative fee, it covers Virginia Organizing's administrative costs, too.

## GETTING SERIOUS AND RAMPING UP

In 2006, State Governing Board Chairperson Janice "Jay" Johnson was ready to "get serious" about organizing. Jay tells the story this way: "VOP was out there doing great campaigns, but we weren't being taken seriously. We needed to figure out a way to get people in power to pay attention to the work we were doing. We had to be everywhere so we would have influence. We needed more people at the local level and we needed to do more statewide campaigns so whoever was a part of the power structure we were targeting would understand that we were everywhere and we were there to stay! VOP also made a big effort to get leaders to talk to elected officials during this shift. We built the local Chapters by recruiting new people, helping them build their own skills, and then getting those leaders to go out and recruit. We ramped up and it paid off!"

## GRASSROOTS FUNDRAISING

Grassroots fundraising was integrated early as an essential element of VOP's work. As Chapters formed, the capacity for working on various issue campaigns grew and the need for workshops increased, so VOP hired more staff – for a total of 12 by January 2007. Staff time was also needed to go train apprentice organizers and interns because experienced organizers were not easily found in Virginia. This is the core of Virginia Organizing – empowering people as leaders to create change in their community. Recruiting and training community organizers and building strong Board members and community leaders are at the heart of Virginia Organizing's work, and doing this important work requires money.

From the very first Organizing Committee meetings to later State Governing Board and staff meetings, fundraising is always a theme at Virginia Organizing. The organization has been creative over the years in applying the principles of diversity to effective fundraising practices. Sound fiscal management, long-term financial management, and general good stewardship of funds raised have always been priorities for VOP, as well as seeing fundraising as a leadership development tool for grassroots leaders, having an ever-expanding individual donor base, recruiting and retaining monthly sustainers, planned giving programs, and developing endowment funds.

### DONOR SPOTLIGHT: SUSAN FRAIMAN

"I am a loyal, long-term donor to Virginia Organizing for several reasons," said Susan Fraiman. "First, I believe strongly in their mission to bring about social justice through community organizing. Second, over the years I have seen concrete evidence of their ability to effect change on a variety of fronts. Third, I have complete trust in their political and fiscal integrity as an organization. I know that their administrative decisions and practices are wholly in keeping with their values. I know that the money I donate is being used wisely and well – for example, to pay every staff member a decent wage without wasting a penny on unnecessary expenses."

Members and leaders are encouraged to be involved not only with their time but also their money. Chapters and leaders have held events like house parties, readings, benefit concerts, yard sales, and silent auctions to provide other opportunities for people to donate. Other less standard fundraising endeavors include participating in programs where a business donates a percentage of a day's sales and collecting items from people to reuse or recycle (ranging from ink cartridges to cars) that can be used by the organization or exchanged for cash. Additionally, at workshops and annual meetings, participants are made aware of the cost of their attendance and encouraged to pay as much as they are able, or to help offset the costs for others who cannot afford to pay. All in all, this approach to fundraising, which mostly relies upon the grassroots efforts of local communities, has sustained Virginia Organizing for 20 years without government funding. The organization has also continuously received funding from various foundations over the years, though the fundraising philosophy has been to increase the donor base and decrease reliance on private foundations.

L.W. and Mo Nichols showed off their soup bowl at the 2012 Social Justice Bowl fundraiser. Local potters donated bowls and area restaurants donated soup and bread to support Virginia Organizing.

Another source of financial support is contracts with national organizations that want Virginia Organizing to organize on specific campaigns in the state. When these contracts make sense in the context of Virginia Organizing's Organizing Plan, they are a welcome source of revenue. However, Virginia Organizing will not accept funds from organizations if the expectations for deliverables are not in line with our Statement of Beliefs and Organizing Plan. (This is not always the case in the non-profit world, as some organizations accept grants for work even when the work does not fit with their goals because funding is needed just for survival.)

## SOCIAL JUSTICE BOWL

From 2004 through 2012, VOP held an annual fundraising event in Charlottesville, the Social Justice Bowl. Virginia potters donated handcrafted bowls; restaurants, caterers, and individuals donated soup, and bakeries donated bread. Annually, a crowd of VOP supporters each selected a bowl, filled it with soup and enjoyed a great evening in which they honored some of VOP's dedicated volunteers and learned more about the organization's work. Attendees could take their bowls home, along with their new knowledge and enthusiasm for VOP.

## STATE TAX REFORM

As all of this organizational development was going on, VOP began serious organizing around state tax reform. As leaders and staff held conversations, meetings, and workshops with a wide range of constituencies over many years, and as Chapters organized around the need for services, a recurring theme kept surfacing: the need in Virginia for a more equitable tax structure that would supply adequate revenue for services.

A national study released in 2002 by the Center for Budget and Policy Priorities ranked Virginia as one of the harshest tax states for working middle-income and working poor families. The study estimated that a single-parent family of three earning $17,661 would owe $483 in Virginia income taxes – the fourth highest figure in the nation, behind Kentucky, Hawaii, and Alabama. At the same time, legislators spent much of the 2002 General Assembly dealing with a $5 billion deficit using an austerity and cuts approach – preserving huge corporate tax breaks and interests and forcing families to make up the shortfall. Many services were cut or eliminated, leaving local governments scrambling to make up – through taxation or additional cuts – for the decrease in state revenue for important public services like law enforcement, schools, infrastructure improvement, and more.

Several commissions appointed by the legislature or the governor made sound recommendations on changes to the tax system, but very few were implemented. VOP developed a "plain and simple language" tax reform campaign that included the following principles:
- Provide appropriate and timely revenue
- Distribute tax burdens equitably
- Promote economic efficiency and growth
- Be easily administered
- Ensure accountability

A diverse statewide strategy committee began making plans, reflecting the VOP approach to combine people who are directly affected by the problems created by unjust policies with people who are experts in the field so that they can all learn from each other. After undertaking a strategic analysis of the key legislators in the state, organizers began to have one-to-one conversations and small meetings in those districts to recruit people to have constituent meetings with the legislators, educate them on tax reform measures and push for their support. More than 75 *Who Pays and Who Benefits?*

workshops, developed and facilitated by VOP leaders and members, were held across the state to teach new people about our state tax system and help them learn about the principles of tax reform that VOP supported. Letters to the editor and op-eds appeared in various media outlets. More than two dozen other organizations joined in the campaign.

Changes were made. In 2003, $7 million was generated by closing the foreign income loophole for royalties and $211 million was saved by stopping the repeal of estate taxes on estates over $1 million. A raise in the state income tax filing threshold from $5,000 to $7,000 for individuals and from $8,000 to $14,000 for married couples meant that 141,000 low-income Virginians were exempt from paying state income taxes. The personal exemption tax credit was increased from $800 to $900 a year and there was a reduction in the sales tax on food.

Working with other allies, VOP helped push for an increase of $1.5 billion in new state support for public education (reducing pressure on local real estate taxes), an increase of $32 million to assist persons with mental disabilities, and the largest infusion of funds for natural resources in Virginia history – $15 million each year to the Water Quality Improvement Fund and $2.5 million per year to the Virginia Land Conservation Foundation.

Organizationally, the tax reform campaign increased VOP's visibility, the number of people participating, and the geographic areas of the organization's influence. It expanded the number of relationships with other groups working for change and increased the level of citizen understanding on issues of tax policy and its impact on local communities and on the working poor. Leaders' and members' relationships with state policymakers were deepened. Finally, the campaign provided VOP leaders and staff with a great learning experience and increased their understanding of the legislature's inner workings that would help increase effectiveness in future campaigns.

"People in general don't like taxes, but none of us really understood why," said Ben Thacker-Gwaltney, the organizer assigned to the campaign. "In this campaign, we were able to show the data and get across the idea that people don't like taxes because we have the sense that they aren't fair. And truly in Virginia, they aren't! The responsibility for most taxes falls on working people, and people of wealth don't pay their fair share. Not even the legislators got this until we started showing them the graphs and doing the 10 Chairs exercise so people could feel the disparity with their bodies." (In the 10 Chairs exercise, you have 10 people and 10 chairs. Each person should make up one tenth of the overall population in the country, but when you get a chair, or a set of chairs, according to your share of the wealth in the country, it is much different. The top person gets about seven chairs, and everyone else is crammed into three chairs on the bottom. The person representing the poorest tenth basically has to stand.)

## EVALUATION

Virginia Organizing uses a process evaluation approach. We maintain an ongoing analysis of our metrics and make modifications to our plans to facilitate successful outcomes.

Evaluation involves the Virginia Organizing State Governing Board and the Virginia Organizing staff. Virginia Organizing holds an annual retreat in November for all Board members and key personnel. Organizational planning includes: fiscal needs, technological improvements, communication standards, leadership and staff development, power analyses, representation in governance, and ongoing evaluation of the organization. In addition, each staff person does a monthly workplan, files a weekly activity report, and does a monthly statistical report to keep track of number of one-to-ones, actions, and other organizing work. Local Chapters and statewide campaign committees develop written strategy plans and revise them as needed.

Responsibility for overall program evaluation rests with the Virginia Organizing State Governing Board, which sets evaluation criteria and expectations for program results. Final program reports document program outcomes. In addition, Virginia Organizing has a system for tracking the activities and accomplishments of organizing and administrative work to provide measurable reports. We keep detailed records of media coverage, workshops, consultations, action alerts and other activities. Virginia Organizing publishes an annual report early in the year and a mid-year report in July or August.

Most groups try to go directly from the problem to the solution. Virginia Organizing has learned that people need to think together (analysis), plan together (Organizing Plan/campaign strategy), act together, and then evaluate together – and then start the cycle over again.

– Excerpt from a funding proposal to The Needmor Fund, 2005

## A SOLID TRACK RECORD

In 10 short years, from its beginnings as a lofty goal in 1995, VOP had established a solid community organizing track record in Virginia by 2005. The organization was working to confront the social and political isolation that accompanies and perpetuates poverty in the state. VOP had provided assistance in the development of new local community organizations addressing economic justice and social justice issues in communities throughout the state, and created a working network of advocacy, faith, labor, housing, education, and other non-profit groups to work together to achieve concrete improvements in such areas as employment, environment, housing and education. VOP had built a solid organizational infrastructure for strategic campaign planning, communications, grassroots leadership development, and fundraising. The stage was set for the second decade of organizing.

# CHAPTER 5
# Expanding Civic Engagement

**MANY EARLY CHAPTERS** held Dismantling Racism workshops soon after forming and many chose campaigns that involved racial disparities in their communities as the early issues they focused on.

Sahar Jawadi, a former Virginia Organizing intern, has a real appreciation for the Dismantling Racism workshops. "The Dismantling Racism workshop was an incredible opportunity to confront systems of oppression," Jawadi said. "I felt better about being able to tackle these societal issues under our group's united front. Sometimes we feel so alone and helpless when we think about all the problems in the world, but when you're in the same room with like-minded, well-intentioned people, you realize that you're not in this alone. As a Muslim woman, I am glad I was able to share my perspective to the group and give them some insight on what's it like to grow up as an American Muslim woman who wears hijab."

Virginia State University students held a 2005 media conference in Petersburg to support legislation to collect data on all police stops in order to fight racial profiling.

Members of Chapters were moved to action as a result of attending Dismantling Racism workshops. For instance, in 2001, the Lynchburg Chapter worked toward replacing the 365-day suspension policy in Lynchburg City Schools with something more flexible, effective, and caring. Under the original policy, children could be suspended for a full year or more for certain violations. The Chapter believed that the children needed more structure and attention in their lives, not less.

In addition, Chapter members wanted to change the biased police-training curriculum in the local Police Academy to include sensitivity and diversity training. Within the context of both of these issue goals, a workshop on Dismantling Racism helped the Chapter members make sense of the underlying causes of the issues: racism in Lynchburg, a long-standing set of behaviors and attitudes that run deep. (Eventually, the Lynchburg Chapter was successful in changing the long-term suspension policy in the city schools so that students receive appropriate alternative education and counseling rather than a mandatory 365-day suspension.)

Additionally, conducting Dismantling Racism workshops and incorporating race into issue campaigns and other discussions remained priorities organization-wide. Even as VOP grew and restructured the Chapter model around legislative districts in order to have more influence on statewide policy, remaining anti-racist stayed in the forefront. Dismantling Racism workshops had become an organizational strength, and many outside groups relied on VOP for them as well. Leaders developed a greater understanding on issues regarding race because these were the issues that affected their communities in so many ways, including access to voting.

## DISMANTLING RACISM TESTIMONY

Tenise Monterio, a Lynchburg Chapter leader, appreciated how a Dismantling Racism workshop helped the Chapter focus on school discipline. "The workshop made us all more aware of racial issues and how we unconsciously participate in furthering racism. And in regard to our campaign against 365 (the school suspension policy), it will make us more sensitive to the fact that this policy is a racist policy."

## EQUAL VOTING RIGHTS

VOP continued to organize more campaigns that relied on legislative action and influencing policy makers. The organization began to look at ways of increasing civic engagement among Virginia's disenfranchised communities and constituencies – those who had lost the right to vote because of past criminal convictions. They talked directly with hundreds of disenfranchised Virginians, a disproportionate number of whom were African-American. As they worked through this process, equal voting rights became very important to the organization.

## PROTECTING THE SECURITY OF ELECTIONS

In 2007, VOP successfully worked with other groups in the Verified Voting Coalition on a campaign to convince the Virginia General Assembly to pass a bill prohibiting future purchases of direct recording electronic voting machines. The new law called for phasing out the machines and replacing them with optical scan voting machines, which provide a paper ballot, giving the voter confidence in the accuracy and security of elections.

The right to vote is a hallmark right in a democracy that claims to want to hear the voices of all its people. Many organized movements in American history have centered on or included a call for voting rights, particularly the Civil Rights Movement and the Women's Suffrage Movement. Yet most modern Virginians were not aware of how many people were still being denied the right to vote. Not only was it important to the work of VOP to have more registered voters be participants in Chapters because of their collective power in legislative issue campaigns, but it was also important in terms of social justice and for the mission of VOP to encourage the participation of the systematically silenced voices.

Since those with prior felony convictions are often disenfranchised, VOP specifically sought them out to push for changes that were important to them. In Virginia, former felons are denied the right to vote based on the type of crime they were charged with and the amount of time that has passed since they completed their sentences; usually, it was a five-to-seven year waiting period before they could even apply for restoration. The governor had the constitutional power to restore civil rights to individuals in Virginia, but in 2001, the restoration process was still lengthy and very complex, and often unsuccessful. The form for some was 13 pages long; a successful application required notarized documents and the participation of a lawyer (both of which were often inaccessible for low-income people), and, once submitted, there was no time limit to how long it would take former felons to hear whether or not their rights would be restored.

In 2002, VOP helped to change this process by organizing people who were directly affected and collaborating with other groups to encourage Governor Mark Warner to improve the process for non-violent offenders. Because of this work, he reduced the application for non-violent offenders to one page, decreased the wait time to three years after release, and promised that applicants would receive a response within six months. Even though automatic restoration upon completion of a person's sentence was the policy change that Virginia Organizing really wanted, this smaller change in the restoration process still greatly increased some people's abilities to regain the right to vote, find their voice, and be full participants in the democratic process.

In 2004, as traction continued with restoration of voter rights and as Chapters continued to participate in issue campaigns based in the legislature, VOP moved toward increasing civic engagement by creating and distributing a non-partisan voter's guide in addition to other voter registration activities. On a local scale, VOP created a local voter's guide for the Charlottesville City Council races. The 16-page guide included information about the general election for City Council, how to register to vote, where to vote, and how to vote by absentee ballot. The main part of the non-partisan guide consisted of answers to 11 questions posed to all six candidates. The local registrar attributed higher voter turnout to the "high caliber" and wide distribution of the voter guide. Given its success, VOP then took this model to the state level and published "No Vote, No Voice," a non-partisan voter registration and education guide, and distributed 90,000 copies statewide through 118 organizations and adult literacy programs.

Other efforts included producing and distributing four public service announcements to 276 radio stations statewide. Well-known civil rights leader Julian Bond recorded the announcements, which focused on voter registration and the process for former felons to seek restoration of their voting rights. VOP also issued e-mail action alerts encouraging Virginians to verify that their voter registration was current and accurate and to inform others of the need to do so. The action alerts included links that provided additional information on voter registration.

These activities were important at the Chapter level as well, where members distributed non-partisan voter guides created by VOP and provided information on voter accessibility for those with special circumstances. The voter guides included information on the new guidelines for restoration of voting and civil rights to former non-violent felons. VOP also worked with college students on get-out-the-vote activities at Virginia State University, the College of William and Mary, and the University of Virginia.

There was a similar non-partisan voter guide published in 2005, when all 100 seats in the House of Delegates, as well as statewide offices for

Governor, Lieutenant Governor, and Attorney General, were up for election in November. VOP members targeted key low-voter-turnout precincts for door-to-door contact and special events. This door-to-door canvassing became a great way to reach new voters and in 2006 became the "Each One Takes Ten" approach, where an individual agreed to make sure 10 people were registered to vote, were fully informed about what is on the ballot, and actually got to the polls. This canvassing effort to reach more people became the catalyst for a much bigger effort in 2008.

Many interns have been trained to do canvassing in local communities.

## BROADER SCALE CIVIC ENGAGEMENT EFFORTS

Preparations began in 2007 for a major door-to-door non-partisan canvass for the summer of 2008. Not only was this effort about reaching more people, but also about bringing groups together in a new way. In 2008, the Virginia Organizing Project took a giant leap forward in organizing Virginians to action, resulting in unprecedented participation in the elections. VOP brought together 13 statewide organizations to form the Virginia C-3 Table (later renamed the Virginia Civic Engagement Table and referred to as "the Table"), a group focused on non-partisan civic engagement activities in the state. It was the first time that most of the largest peoples' organizations in Virginia came together in a formal way for a common purpose. This coalition grew and by 2010, the Virginia Civic Engagement Table was made up of 25 non-partisan groups across the state that were devoted to voter participation.

A large part of the early work of the Table was the 2008 Summer Civic Engagement Project. Under this successful program, VOP hired 50 interns, who, along with hundreds of volunteers, knocked on more than 140,000 doors across the state. All together, with help from other groups in the Virginia C-3 Table, 300,000 copies of a 32-page non-partisan voter guide that VOP developed were distributed. The VOP interns received a living wage and a priceless education!

Other Table activities that year included notifying the Virginia Department of Social Services (DSS) that it was not in compliance with the National Voter Registration Act of 1993, causing DSS to make major improvements in its voter registration systems. VOP worked with other organizations – Demos, Virginia NAACP, Project Vote, Democracy South – to make this important change. Additionally, the Table conducted voter protection training and get-out-the-vote activities that included distributing non-partisan door hangers and voter empowerment cards, phone banking, distributing voter information through small businesses and on college campuses, tabling at public events, and giving people rides to the polls. Turnout percentages for underrepresented constituencies went up substantially in the precincts where the efforts were focused.

VOP used all forms of technology and media to get out the vote: paper and digital copies of voter guides, tabling at events, radio ads, physical door-to-door canvassing, a blog for the summer canvassers to post their "Front Porch Diaries," and phone banking. The summer project the next year (2009) brought similar success as VOP published and distributed 275,000 copies of "Virginia Votes 2009: Your Guide to the Virginia Elections," another 32-page non-partisan voter guide. Along with canvassing 155,679 doors across the state to distribute these guides, VOP interns also collected 1,183 used cell phones and printer cartridges for recycling and registered 360 people to vote. In addition, interns and members were able to talk with residents about priority issues and health care reform as a part of VOP's new health care campaign.

The 2008 and 2009 summer civic engagement projects were also the perfect place to show VOP's members and leaders, along with all Virginia residents, where two major campaigns – civic engagement and health care reform – came together. These civic engagement projects reflected the importance of Virginia Organizing's continued efforts to be non-partisan and multi-issue, while maintaining a diverse constituency.

Summer interns canvassed and conducted one-to-one conversations in many communities to register voters and create photo petitions to send to U.S. Senators Jim Webb and Mark Warner. The photos, like the one above of Ernest Williams in Danville, helped people express their need for jobs in their communities in support of the Local Jobs for America Act. VOP found that many people facing difficult economic circumstances would prefer not to focus on politics, but they were willing and excited to do the photo petition, make phone calls, and encourage friends to do the same because this bill could change their everyday lives.

Canvassers also asked what issues people were most concerned about and gave out flyers on climate change and health care, depending on the area in which they lived, encouraging people to contact their state legislators about these issues. In addition to the voter education work, the interns recruited volunteers to participate in the canvass and register people to vote. Adventures included five dog bites (none serious), six flat tires, a major heat wave, and a tornado! Interns tried out new techniques as well, like having one of the teams doing a targeted phone bank in northern Virginia to ensure that Latino/a communities were given the opportunity to register to vote. In Danville and Southwest Virginia, three canvassers handed out compact fluorescent light bulbs in low-income communities of color after hearing people describe over and over the high energy rates charged in their town. In South Hampton Roads, the focus was on registering voters in African-American communities. Interns canvassing in a very rural part of Scott County (southwest Virginia) who weren't getting much of a response called a local VOP Chapter member, who told them that everyone in the area gathered at a local diner. They set up a table there for a few days, recruiting volunteers and generating calls to their state Delegate's office about the need for health care access for all Virginians. Teams worked festivals, fairs, and fish fries with great success, mostly in small towns and rural areas, handing out voter education materials and expanding VOP's visibility in the public.

However, after doing expanded non-partisan civic engagement work in 2008 (a presidential election year in which Virginia became a battleground state) and 2009 (an election for statewide offices of governor, lieutenant governor, and attorney general), Virginia Organizing's analysis was that further large-scale voter registration and canvassing did not make sense for the organization. Large-scale canvassing didn't turn out to be very conducive for long-term organizational capacity building. Leaders of the organization felt that civic engagement work would be most effective when it was tied to local organizing and Chapters; VOP wants people to be active all year round, every year!

### INTEGRATING A LEGISLATIVE APPROACH

VOP understood that it needed a multi-pronged approach to working with the state legislature to raise the voices of directly affected people and to empower constituents to hold their elected officials accountable beyond Election Day. In 2007, the State Governing Board adopted a four-pronged approach to legislative work: VOP State Governing Board members would lobby in Richmond on behalf of the organization; veteran lobbyist Ben Greenberg, the legislative coordinator, would lobby full-time during the legislative session on behalf of VOP; Chapter leaders would visit their legislators in Richmond while the General Assembly was in session; and there would be targeted phone calls and e-mails from constituents on particular issues. Over time, VOP shifted to meeting with legislators primarily back in their home districts throughout the year to leverage the power of constituents and give leaders more of an opportunity to meet with legislators.

Virginia Organizing continues to expand non-partisan civic engagement activities across the Commonwealth by getting all the Chapters to push for more involvement in the political process, especially by low-income people, youth, unmarried women, and people of color, through voter registration, issue education, and get-out-the-vote activities. Virginia Organizing also still recruits volunteers to do phone banking all year to contact targeted constituencies to take action on specific issues.

One of the key goals throughout the year is to identify opportunities to connect issue work and to move voters to action in a variety of ways. Instead of just registering a voter and then hoping they show up on election day, VOP resolved to try to get new registrants active in a Chapter, offering a wide variety of leadership development and political education opportunities throughout the year, and helped them to connect to lots of other people in their own community.

Virginia Organizing's job is to help Virginians realize their true potential as participants in a democracy, and the promise that ordinary people and their concerns really do matter. The goal is to help people create durable power – non-partisan power – they can use to fashion a more fair, just Virginia over time.

# CHAPTER 6

# Being a Part of National Health Care Reform

IN 2008, VOP'S POWER analysis pointed to adding health care as a priority issue. Because of the organization's growing capacity across the state, VOP was selected as the lead organization for Health Care for America Now! (HCAN) efforts in Virginia.

Health care laws have been changing for a long, long time in the United States. After many years of reforms and attempts at reform of the market-driven, for-profit health care industrial system, politicians began to look at universal coverage options on par with other developed nations. During the presidency of Bill Clinton, there was an attempt to pass universal health care in Congress. Unfortunately, due to the complexity of the law, mistrust in government programs by the public, and a Congress unwilling to address the issue of health care reform, nothing passed at the time.

In 2008, President Barack Obama saw an opportunity to make health care reform a reality and worked with Congress to get a bill written and passed in 2010. The Patient Protection and Affordable Care Act (ACA) ended up being a compromise bill that provided a vehicle for health care for most people while maintaining the existing private market. The law provided subsidies and expanded Medicaid to ensure that everyone could afford care and included an individual mandate to guarantee that almost everyone would have health insurance coverage.

The real fight for health care reform was not only in Washington but also in local communities across the nation, where grassroots leaders worked to build support for quality, affordable health care for all. For VOP's part in the health care effort, the State Governing Board created a statewide strategy committee early in 2008 to decide how to move the state and nation toward access to quality, affordable health care for all, the overall campaign goal. The first tasks the strategy committee took on were finding directly affected people, building public awareness, and involving more people in the campaign.

Because of the strong, powerful grassroots base that had remained multi-issue, multi-constituency, and well-connected with other groups, meetings with legislators about any issue were much more productive and had great depth. In one instance, along with four other groups, VOP met with the Speaker of the Virginia House of Delegates to discuss policy priorities for 2009. While health care was a key reason for the meeting, the conversation also turned to public education issues, environmental concerns, and the need to increase wages for personal care assistants, as VOP leaders demonstrated that they were knowledgeable on a wide range of issues and could work collectively and effectively with other groups. The Speaker understood that VOP and other groups knew the complexity of issues, cared about Virginians, and were not organized for one issue or one campaign, but for long-term change for the good of all Virginians.

Opportunities like this meeting also helped VOP in other ways besides legislation, enhancing relations with other groups and allowing for teaching moments and development of new leadership skills for members. In a large meeting, like those with elected officials, VOP's selection of speakers and leaders in the room was always strategic. Typically, there were directly affected people prepared to talk about their experience with the issues, along with a combination of experienced leaders and people new to the organization so that they could learn from one another. Overall, the experience was much less intimidating for the new people because of the presence of those with experience. This strategy is still employed for many organizing activities at Virginia Organizing, ranging from media conferences to legislator meetings to direct actions to leading Chapter meetings. The emphasis on relationship building and leadership development means that over time the leaders are the ones doing these development activities with one another – conducting one-to-one conversations, sharing their stories, teaching others to write letters to the editor, running Chapter meetings, and planning actions and activities.

As for HCAN, some other health care reform activities where VOP served as the lead organization included: garnering congressional support for HCAN health care reform principles, holding local forums to keep the issue relevant at the community level, conducting interviews of directly affected people, tracking health care stories, having people write letters to the editor and op-eds, doing phone banking, and mailing postcards to Members of Congress. Work for health care reform (which is still going on at the time of this writing as Virginia Organizing works to encourage the state legislature to expand Medicaid) has been an action-oriented campaign.

For example, in 2008, VOP held an action outside Anthem's corporate headquarters in Richmond to encourage the company to be a part of the health care solution. The action came after 10 weeks of knocking on tens of thousands of doors in every corner of the Commonwealth. During this canvassing, VOP asked people what is the most important issue they face in their communities. Thousands of Virginians talked about the lack of affordable accessible health care and VOP wanted to make sure Anthem – the state's largest insurer – heard those concerns.

Virginia State University students showed their support for health care reform in 2009 outside the Benedict Club in Petersburg.

In 2009, VOP leaders held a variety of events, including a series of rush-hour events at Falls Church Metro stops to encourage commuters to call

Congressman Gerry Connolly and Senator Mark Warner, asking them to support the public health insurance option. A VOP newsletter at the time described the action this way: "Event organizers had a life-sized cardboard cutout of Congressman Connolly to make sure that at least the two dimensional version of him is listening to the concerns of his constituents and not of the insurance industry lobby."

Later in 2009, Fredericksburg VOP leaders donning Santa hats gathered outside the Fredericksburg library and asked local residents to sign a "Snowflake Petition" by writing their health care stories and concerns on snowflake ornaments later delivered to Senators Mark Warner and Jim Webb.

The most important aspect of these actions was that they were planned and led by directly affected people and only happened with local support and when they made sense for a local Chapter; VOP's intention was to build the local Chapters and help local people develop as stronger leaders. For example, in Charlottesville, Dell Erwin frequently spoke out about the need for health care reform because her grandson had a serious pre-existing condition that would disqualify him from insurance in the future and could mean that he would eventually exhaust lifetime limits on his insurance policies. Since the ACA removed discrimination for pre-existing conditions and eliminated lifetime limits on the amount insurance companies would pay out, her grandson benefited directly.

"Health care is needed by everyone and should be a right, not a privilege," said Erwin. "Thanks to the ACA, I got help when I was in the 'donut hole' (the gap in Medicare prescription coverage) during cancer treatment. Because of the ACA, millions more have health insurance and millions more have better health care." Her story, like hundreds of others, was incredibly important to put a human face on the real struggle that people had before the ACA became law.

"In my six years with Virginia Organizing, I am proudest of the role we played in health care reform because of what we did in terms of community service, leadership development, and public information," said Winston Whitehurst, a leader in Virginia Organizing's statewide health care reform strategy committee and in the South Hampton Roads Chapter. "From the very introduction of the Affordable Care Act, I participated in prayer vigils, petitioned legislators, served on public informational programs, wrote letters to newspaper editors, and talked on radio and television programs, all supporting the passage of health care reforms.

"While the Patient Protection and Affordable Care Act has been a century in the making, its passage was a milestone," Whitehurst added.

## SOME BENEFITS – AND CHALLENGES – OF CONNECTING TO A NATIONAL CAMPAIGN

For VOP, getting active in a national campaign meant looking at current practices and ensuring that the organizational philosophy aligned with the issue campaign values. HCAN provided an opportunity to put the bottom-up organizing model to the test on a major national issue, while keeping to core principles of the Statement of Beliefs and the Organizing Plan. It is important to maintain the values of the organization when choosing to partner with any other group, but especially national groups. National groups are typically well-funded and have their own agendas that often do not include leadership development and building strategic capacity for long-term community organizing. In a national campaign, it helps to take the strengths of the approach of the national group(s) and combine it with the strengths of the local/statewide group. In the era of top-down short-term organizing that relies mostly on producing deliverables, Virginia Organizing has remained bottom-up. The organization has remained committed to the community, trusting that people of different backgrounds – race, class, sexual orientation, etc. – can come together to create their own change without blindly following the directives of a national effort with strict policy change goals. By partnering with HCAN, Virginia Organizing was able to connect to a very visible campaign, share in the momentum of a critical national issue, gain more insight on key federal elected officials to target, and maintain a core organizing focus: empower people to raise their voices to "speak truth to power" and make a big difference.

The national health care campaign also came with some challenges. What was meant to be a one-year campaign went on much longer. Also, local and statewide groups had very little to say about the actual content and the timing of the legislation that resulted from organizing efforts.

On other issue campaigns, the national groups would sometimes ask for deliverables that met their own objectives while doing little to build the organization and ongoing efforts of groups like VOP. When faced with these challenges, because VOP was structured to be independent of national funding, the organization was in a better position to negotiate for deliverables and campaign goals that made sense for Virginians.

## VISIBILITY

Visibility is also an important part of statewide community organizing. With the summer civic engagement canvassing projects and expansion into the national arena for various campaigns like health care reform, the Virginia Organizing Project greatly increased its public presence. The organization was featured multiple times in 2009-2010 in a series on National Public Radio that spotlighted community organizing. The series included reflections from VOP representatives on the changes that had occurred since the Obama administration took office. VOP leaders shared their realistic expectations and understanding of the long, complicated process of social and economic change.

Additionally, VOP members attended national summits, led trainings at national gatherings, met elected and appointed officials at the federal level, and increased their media presence in local, state, and national settings through letters to the editor, op-eds, and media releases. Since Virginia Organizing works with grassroots leaders and directly affected people as spokespeople in the media, every media hit means people learn new skills or deepen existing ones. As Virginia Organizing worked on national issues, more national and even international media coverage followed. While media attention is not what guides organizing, good community organizing creates media spokespeople as Chapters are developed, more people take action, and leaders grow.

The work with HCAN and other national groups was not without appropriate tension and challenges, but it also provided an opportunity for leaders to learn about national campaigns and grow more, and for VOP to be a part of national policies that were affecting real people in Virginia every single day. Through long-term relationship building with national groups, Virginia Organizing has been able to participate in national campaigns and remain focused on the needs and strengths of the local Chapters and leaders. Virginia Organizing did this by continuing to ask the important questions about relationships with national groups: does this make sense for local leaders in local Chapters?

HCAN ended its work in 2013, but because Virginia Organizing had the capacity on the ground and had built a sustainable organization through diverse fundraising, the organization was able to continue fighting for health care needs of Virginians without resources from HCAN.

CHAPTER 7

# Changing the Name but Not the Work

IN 2010, THE VIRGINIA ORGANIZING PROJECT became Virginia Organizing as a result of a reflection process generously donated by Hairpin Communications, a national firm that specializes in helping social change organizations with messaging and public relations. The VOP State Governing Board wondered what Virginians thought of the organization after all these years and asked the firm to research the question. After conducting focus groups within the organization and a wide range of interviews with other community leaders, elected officials, and representatives of a variety of social change groups, Hairpin concluded that VOP was solid in its mission and identity and that people associate the organization with tenacity, integrity, and justice, but they did not always know what the Virginia Organizing Project did. The goal of providing clarity to how the organization

Young grassroots leaders showed off the new logo and name.

presents itself on a larger stage was to establish its permanence, whereas the word "project" made it sound like a temporary venture, as well as to clearly identify the grassroots approach to change. The Board voted to shorten the name to Virginia Organizing and decided that the full name would be used all the time – no acronyms.

"The name changes, but not the work," Chairperson Sandra A. Cook wrote in the 2010 annual report. "The logo changes, but not the people." It was also around this time that community organizing had gained significant media attention and popularity due to President Barack Obama's own history as an organizer and the use of organizing tactics in his campaigns. Because President Obama had worked as a community organizer in Chicago for three years in the 1980s before his political career, people were curious about the field. Because national campaigns and organizations saw the Obama campaign tactics work, they sought to replicate them in their own work. Virginia Organizing wanted people to understand that "campaign organizing" is about short-term goals and temporary organizing, but the deeper "community organizing" that Virginia Organizing does is about long-term change and endurance.

The new national emphasis on campaign-focused organizing relied on an idea about who had influential power that could be levied from a national policy perspective; national groups sent in organizers to densely populated areas to produce deliverables – sometimes misguided – such as number of phone bank calls, turnout to events and actions, and media hits and coverage. While these are elements of organizing that may be helpful for certain campaigns, a lot is lost when an organizer drops into a community for a few months to follow directives from a national group or campaign and then disappears when funding runs out. Big national campaigns let people down when they are done and leave the area; grassroots community organizing strengthens communities and brings new people together to work to better the community in the long run. Virginia Organizing is willing to work with national campaigns only when the work makes sense in terms of building long-term power and strategic capacity.

## FINANCIAL REFORM

Around 2010, the same year as the name change, Virginia Organizing became active in a different level of policy change that affected many Americans: financial reform legislation to increase transparency about big business and prioritize the financial security of small local businesses. This was a part of a larger struggle between "Main Street" and "Wall Street" and the work for this win happened alongside work for other issues like a tax reform effort called "Balance Virginia!," efforts to bring local jobs to communities in Virginia as a part of the Local Jobs for America Act, and opposing the state legislature's efforts to ban the implementation of the Affordable Care Act, which had recently passed. These state and national efforts, while focused on different aspects of people's lives, were a part of the strategic push that year to help communities understand the intersections of these different issues. Health care reform affects job creation and small business success, and increased local jobs affect the local and state economy. Getting people involved in critical thinking about these issues helps build power for the organization and develops stronger leaders.

Executive Director Joe Szakos paused to speak to the media before entering the courtroom for his trial. Szakos was arrested at Anthem's Richmond headquarters in 2009 when a group of Virginia Organizing leaders wanted to ask why the organization's health insurance premiums increased by 14 percent. Anthem employees refused to let them in the main door of the corporate headquarters and called the police. All charges were eventually dropped.

## MORE TECHNOLOGY, MORE VISIBILITY

By the end of 2010, Virginia Organizing moved into a new technological era. Staff were equipped with FlipCams to capture video at actions and upload those to YouTube. Virginia Organizing also updated the website and began using many social media tools still in use today like Facebook, Twitter, YouTube, and Flickr. These tools were helpful when Executive Director Joe Szakos was arrested outside of Anthem headquarters in Richmond after approaching the building with State Governing Board members – during business hours – to ask why the organization's premiums had risen more than 14 percent that year. While others demonstrated on the sidewalk outside, the group of four people approached the main door to talk to someone in customer service, but the main door had been locked. Even though they were told to wait for Anthem customer service personnel, and were doing so, the police were called. The group was told to leave; Szakos refused and was arrested for criminal trespassing. The charges were later dropped.

The arrest and subsequent media conferences were recorded and uploaded to Virginia Organizing's YouTube page, website, and other social media sharing sites, and were used in national media reports. Virginia Organizing used these techniques to help inform people about the problems consumers faced with the insurance industry. The arrest showed the world an example of an insurance company that cares more about profits than people. The dismissal of charges showed Virginians that big corporations do not have all the power and that people and our voices matter – even on issues that initially seem too big to tackle.

## STAFF DEVELOPMENT

One of the most important elements of Virginia Organizing's work, leadership development, is possible because of the relationship-building efforts of committed community organizers. That's why the organization invests significant time and resources to ensure their successful professional development. Early on, solid staff benefits were set up to encourage staff to stay longer and to prevent burnout. The State Governing Board truly places "family first" for staff and practices this commitment on a regular basis by providing health and dental insurance, vacation and other time off, sabbaticals, retirement, paid parental leave, child care, and other benefits. These staff benefits are an embodiment of how the organization upholds its Statement of Beliefs and what it would like to see available for all Virginians. Virginia Organizing continues to operate under the belief that all staff should be developing just as leaders are. Every year, staff submit self-development plans and receive paid time off and a stipend to accomplish their developmental goals. After five years, staff people earn a one-month sabbatical (and two months after ten years) to deepen their development, refresh and renew, and learn new skills for organizing. This culture of life-long learning allows staff to gain new skills to be better at their jobs while continuing to grow the organization. Without committed and supported community organizers and other staff, Virginia Organizing would not have become the statewide force that it is today.

## FIGHTING FOR RESTORATION OF VOTING RIGHTS

In 2010, Virginia Organizing and other civil rights and faith groups united to encourage then Governor Tim Kaine to sign an executive order to restore voting rights for all of Virginia's disenfranchised felons prior to leaving office. The groups shared their message via media, lobby meetings, letters to the editor, and thousands of phone calls generated to the Governor's office. Virginia Organizing's South Hampton Roads Chapter held a phone bank and waffle breakfast, encouraging Governor Kaine to "stop waffling and sign the Executive Order." Governor Kaine ultimately declined to sign an Executive Order. While the decision was dis-appointing, new members got involved and the issue received significant national attention. By 2015, Virginia Organizing had made more headway under Governors Bob

Virginia Governor Terry McAuliffe spoke to Fredericksburg leader Eunice Haigler after his June 2015 announcement to remove out-standing fines and court fees as a barrier to restoration of voting rights. While the fees and fines still must be paid, they no longer prevent someone from gaining back the right to vote after a felony conviction.

McDonnell and Terry McAuliffe. The restoration of rights process is more streamlined and automated, the application is shorter, the requirement of payment of court costs and fees are removed, and more people are able to get their rights back faster than ever before. This is because of the work of Virginia Organizing and other groups and building relationships with the Governors' key staff people.

# CHAPTER 8

# A Strong Grassroots Force

**VIRGINIA ORGANIZING HAD BECOME** a strong grassroots force in Virginia by 2011. State and national campaigns frequently looked to Virginia Organizing to provide direction for campaigns throughout the state. A big part of most of these national efforts was a combination of educating people and helping communities uncover the root causes of some of the issues that were affecting their daily lives – issues Virginia Organizing was already addressing.

Leaders from the Charlottesville, Danville, and Martinsville/Henry County Chapters held a "Pay Your Fair Share" protest and sit-in at U.S. Representative Robert Hurt's Danville district office to highlight the need for tax reform and a fairer budget.

For instance, Virginia Organizing continued to work to implement the new national health care reforms by empowering people who were positively affected by the changes to tell their stories: young people who were finally allowed to stay on their parents' insurance policies until the age of 26 and individuals who were able to get health insurance for the first time in their lives because of pre-existing conditions.

Economics education and understanding how government works have always been a large part of Virginia Organizing's work, whether that means helping people understand the state and federal budget, or teaching them about the regressive structure of the tax systems in our society.

## AMERICANS FOR TAX FAIRNESS

Other state and national campaigns in which Virginia Organizing participated were determined by how those campaigns fit with the local work of the Chapters. The Danville Chapter became involved with the national push for job creation because of the high unemployment rate that was creating excessive hardship for many people in Danville. In addition, the Danville

Chapter leaders were fed up with wealthy individuals and corporations paying such a low percentage of federal tax dollars (corporations paid just 12.6 percent of worldwide income in U.S. taxes in 2010 according to CNN Money) when those individuals and corporations were often the ones to reap the most rewards from government investment in infrastructure, education, and public safety.

**"THANK TAXES"**

Virginia Organizing's Charlottesville Chapter celebrated the 2011 Tax Day by thanking taxes for things like police officers, roads, schools, water systems, social services, and more. A part of this rally was to inform people about what their taxes actually pay for and to help them understand the value they get for the taxes they pay. Long-time Virginia Organizing supporter and Chapter leader Jane Foster is pictured here.

Jane Foster, a dedicated Charlottesville Chapter leader, showed her support for taxes by highlighting what taxes accomplish in her local community.

Chapter leaders in other communities were appalled that school budgets were being cut while federal tax dollars were paying for a fighter jet that had been in production for many years, cost trillions of dollars, and was not going to be "mission ready" for many more years. This kind of excessive government waste was troublesome for families who wanted a good education system for all the children in the community.

Virginia Organizing recognized that those who benefited from tax loopholes were not necessarily to blame: the lawmakers who created the loopholes and caved to lobbyists and corporate donors had the primary responsibility for them. When Virginia Organizing partnered with Americans for Tax Fairness to highlight the needs of a fairer tax structure that works for all people, it was because it made sense at the local level to move in that direction. Danville and many other Virginia localities were suffering because of federal budget cuts and companies shipping jobs overseas. The national work on tax fairness was not about policy to most local people; it was about their everyday lives.

## BUSTING UP BIG BANKS

During the economic boom of the late 1990s and early 2000s, big banks engaged in egregiously reckless financial behavior, putting the entire world's economy in peril. The biggest banks were betting against the average American family, taking on bad debt they knew families could not afford to repay, repackaging that bad debt, and selling it off to make money. Bad banking practices, expansion of subprime mortgages, and high consumer debt caused the stock market to crash and plunged the United States into the Great Recession. While unemployment rose, the federal government bailed out some of those banks with the worst practices in order to keep the economy from totally collapsing. People in Virginia were feeling that pressure and economic insecurity. At the same time, big banks were still underwriting payday loans and actively using predatory lending practices to target people of color and other protected classes.

Virginia Organizing found an effective local way to combat the big banks – divesting! Chapter leaders and their families, friends, and neighbors took as many of their assets as possible from the large banks and switched to local banks and credit unions that were a part of the community. Local banks are generally more responsive to the communities they serve while large banks are accountable to shareholders for turning a profit, sometimes to the detriment of everyday people. Virginia Organizing remained consistent by working strategically to develop Chapter leaders, connecting to national campaigns through local work that made sense to Chapters, and continuing to raise the voices of directly affected people.

Virginia Organizing protested the bad banking practices of Bank of America and other big Wall Street banks at shareholder meetings and at bank locations across Virginia in 2012.

## AFFORDABLE HEALTH CARE

The specific action plans for state and national issue campaigns varied depending on the issue. Sometimes it was important to organize people to leverage the power of their group and let legislators or other elected officials know what constituents specifically wanted and needed. This meant sharing stories, making phone calls, and holding meetings to learn from other directly affected people and ensure that all voices were being heard by elected officials.

But when there was no clear demand set by a coordinated campaign effort, other issues called for strategies like workshops to educate people on the nuances of an issue, or forums to provide an opportunity for people to brainstorm about solutions to problems or changes they want to see in their communities. Workshops and forums led to action planning and community members developing their own clear demands. One example of this was the work Virginia Organizing did in the wake of the U.S. Supreme Court ruling upholding most of the ACA in 2012.

In 2012, the ACA had been challenged in court by several states. The Supreme Court heard arguments for and against the individual mandate portion of the law, Medicaid expansion, and other elements of the ACA. That June, the Court ruled in favor of most of the provisions of the ACA, but ruled that states could not be required to expand Medicaid under the threat of losing current Medicaid funding. Medicaid expansion became optional for states, and in the states that did not expand Medicaid, people who earned below 100 percent of the federal poverty limit but earned too much for their current state's Medicaid program, this meant continued reliance on free clinics, emergency rooms, and charity care – and a corresponding lack of preventive services like having a regular physician and getting regular check ups. Reactive medicine is always more expensive than prevention, which is one reason Medicaid expansion was so important as a cost saving measure.

Instead of having major rallies in the state capital, Virginia Organizing has found it more effective to hold multiple, simultaneous events in different media markets and legislative districts across the state. Chapter leaders in Southwest Virginia and the Virginia Education Association gathered to hold one of nine statewide vigils to support Medicaid expansion in Virginia in 2014.

When the ACA was passed, it was done with the understanding that Medicaid would be expanded in the states to cover individuals and families who fall at 138 percent of the federal poverty level or below. Because federal taxes would pay for Medicaid expansion, states would only ever be required to pay 10 percent of the cost of the new enrollees. The ACA was written with the assumption that expansion would happen not only because of the consequences to states that did not expand, but also because it is a really good financial deal for states. The authors of the ACA only created a subsidy for those who earned between 100 and 400 percent of the federal poverty level if purchasing insurance through the Health Insurance Marketplace because of this assumption.

When the Supreme Court ruled that states' current Medicaid funding could not be revoked if they failed to expand Medicaid, hundreds of thousands of Virginians suddenly found themselves in what was coined the "Medicaid coverage gap"–their income was too high or they did not meet other criteria to qualify for Virginia's restrictive Medicaid program, but they earned too little to qualify for a federal subsidy in the Marketplace under the ACA. Thus, people who were working in low-paying fields, sometimes at multiple jobs to make ends meet, were left without an option for health insurance. This painful reality touched Virginia Organizing leaders and members and many of them found either that they themselves fell in the coverage gap or knew someone who did. Since 2009, all

Fredericksburg resident Eunice Haigler talks about her experiences with treatment for a brain tumor and the lack of Medicaid funding during a Virginia Organizing media conference to support Medicaid expansion in Virginia in 2014. (Photo credit: Robert A. Martin/ Freelance)

Chapters have participated in health care organizing. Chapters held vigils, gatherings, and other actions for Medicaid expansion. Eunice Haigler of Fredericksburg got active in the fall of 2013, after the law was passed and the Supreme Court made a decision on Medicaid, but before the ACA's Health Insurance Marketplace was rolled out. Haigler frequently spoke out at media conferences and other actions because she fell into the Medicaid coverage gap. Because of Haigler's lack of health insurance before the ACA, she became partially blind. She has been fighting since the ACA passed to get coverage for herself and other Virginians in the Medicaid coverage gap. Virginia Organizing focused on both changing the system to ensure access to Medicaid and working within the system to get eligible people signed up for health insurance under the new law. Like other directly affected people, Eunice is now a core member of the Fredericksburg Chapter and has organized campaigns on voting rights and the "school to prison" pipeline.

When the ACA enrollment began in late 2013, as with any large program rollout that relied on technology as a large portion of the program, there were glitches. Some politicians who were adamantly against the ACA used the moment to attack the program and advocated for repeal of the law without any other solution for the millions of people who needed health insurance but would lose it without the vital protections of the law or the insurance marketplace the law created.

"It was a real shame," said Virginia Organizing Board member Ray Scher. "Politicians were so focused on what they didn't like about the ACA that they would not see the needs of real Virginians. People were suffering because they could not access Medicaid expansion, but Virginia's legislators failed them."

Virginia Organizing again looked to more localized solutions to national problems. In South Hampton Roads and Richmond, the Chapters decided to invite Virginia's Regional Director for the federal Department of Health and Human Resources, Joanne Grossi, to present information about the benefits of the law, what to expect with rollout, and how the ACA could insure many more Americans.

In the South Hampton Roads Chapter presentation with Grossi, a state legislator from the Shenandoah Valley drove to Virginia Beach to gather information. When he learned more about the benefits of Medicaid expansion and the need for full implementation of the law, he became a proponent of expansion, against the wishes of his political party. The South Hampton Roads Chapter went on to partner with the Virginia Beach Department of Health to do dozens of community enrollment fairs to make sure that Virginians received guidance when applying for health insurance through the federal Health Insurance Marketplace, in addition to continuing to organize for Medicaid expansion.

Although the political climate in Richmond, the state capital, still makes Medicaid expansion unlikely, many legislators have been touched by the stories of hard-working Virginians being left out of the system. Unfortunately, their political partisanship and ambition outweigh their own conviction.

## BUILDING A STRONG GRASSROOTS POLITICAL FORCE

Along with coordinated, statewide efforts for policy change and raising consciousness about the issues, Virginia Organizing continued to organize local issue campaigns. Often, those in positions of power make decisions that affect entire communities without gaining input or consent from them. For instance, there were environmental concerns in southside and eastern Virginia communities about potential uranium mining and rail cars storing explosive and toxic chemicals in a Fredericksburg neighborhood posed a threat to people's health and lives. Virginia Organizing identified these issues through one-to-one conversations, worked to educate residents in communities about these concerns and then organized with people to ensure that their voices were being heard by those who could make decisions to change the outcome. During this same time in Williamsburg, at the College of William and Mary, students conducted a sit-in to

VOP supported students at the University of Virginia who organized to demand a living wage there in Spring 2006.

encourage university administrators to raise the wages of the college's lowest paid workers. There had been much larger pushes for living wages at other universities in the past, but different communities have different issue focuses depending on what is affecting people the most, the political climate, and current events.

Building a strong grassroots force enabled Virginia Organizing to focus on what made sense to different Chapters at different times. While all Chapters participated in health care reform organizing, each Chapter had its own focus and unique perspective. Chapters that worked on living wage campaigns, for example, did so when the issue was ripe for change in their community. The benefit to this approach is that Chapter leaders are able to be creative and work on what makes sense to their community while still contributing to building the power of the organization. Virginia Organizing learned the importance of local Chapters determining what made sense during national campaigns and that focus led to unwavering commitment to leadership development and local Chapter building.

## RULE OF THREE

Virginia Organizing often uses the "Rule of Three" at media conferences. Person One, who has never spoken to an audience before, builds confidence just from stepping to the podium and introducing Person Two, who is still relatively inexperienced at public speaking, but builds that leadership skill while holding the media conference, and Person Three, who is well versed on the subject being discussed and can field most any question. Virginia Organizing intentionally uses these kinds of leadership ladders to develop more grassroots leaders.

CHAPTER 9

# Organizing on a Variety of Issues

## CSX RAIL CARS IN FREDERICKSBURG

The Fredericksburg Chapter worked with local residents to oppose CSX's storing of rail cars containing toxic materials in the middle of a residential neighborhood. Senator Edd Houck successfully proposed a budget amendment that called for CSX to move their cars through residential neighborhoods in Fredericksburg/Spotsylvania within eight hours or lose $42 million in state funding for a variety of rail programs. The rail cars were being stored in areas of economic poverty.

**VIRGINIA ORGANIZING'S STATEMENT OF BELIEFS**, input from local Chapters, and guidance of the State Governing Board help determine what issues make sense to tackle in addition to Chapters' identified needs and issues. To begin to improve people's lives and build power for social change, Virginia Organizing helps them understand that fighting for environmental issues intersects with better health care, which intersects with wages and employment, which intersects with supporting local businesses, and so forth.

In 2011, Virginia Organizing hired an organizer whose job was working with small businesses to help determine what issues were important to them and affecting them and the people in their community. This project was known as the Virginia Main Street Alliance. Organizing small business owners to raise their voices was effective when the Virginia General Assembly was debating the health insurance marketplace. Virginia Organizing provided a space for small businesses to define and describe what the marketplace should look like for them and helped small business leaders set up meetings with their legislators to communicate their needs. The General Assembly ultimately decided that Virginians would use the federal Health Insurance Marketplace instead of setting up a state-specific plan. Small business owners continued to organize in support of Medicaid expansion and spoke out against national attempts to repeal "Obamacare" (a nickname given to the ACA by its opponents and eventually embraced by its supporters). Eventually, instead of considering small business leaders as a separate constituency, they were integrated into the multi-constituency approach at the Chapter level to strengthen local Chapters.

## LOCAL ORGANIZING CONTINUES

National campaigns continued to want to partner with Virginia Organizing, but the Board was selective about these partnerships in order to remain true to the foundation of the organization and to grassroots community organizing. Virginia Organizing continued the local issue work during national campaigns, organizing around such issues as affordable housing, drug courts, accessibility to public buildings, human rights, predatory lending, and education.

Another example of local issue organizing was anti-racism work, which has always been a part of Virginia Organizing. Not a year has gone by without Dismantling Racism workshops. In local communities and state-wide, the effects of racism surface in different ways. In the South Hampton Roads area, the Chapter made sure to speak up for fair ward redistricting to prevent gerrymandering when that issue arose in Norfolk. Race issues on the local, state, and national scale are as important to Virginia Organizing leaders today as they were in 1995 when the Organizing Committee chose to intentionally address racism.

## VOTER ID LAWS

When the Virginia General Assembly was proposing new voter ID laws, Virginia Organizing spoke out against these attempts to increase barriers to voting. Local, state, and federal redistricting, voter ID laws, and other voting policies affect people of color in significant ways and the historical abuses of power by white power structures must be considered when creating these laws and policies. Virginia Organizing organized with people of color and allies to raise concerns to those who were making the decisions in hopes that change could happen through these actions. Virginia Organizing found that not all decision-makers chose to listen or provide access or forums for directly affected individuals to express their thoughts, share their stories, and hold lawmakers accountable. This led Virginia Organizing to coalesce with others who wished to change the level of transparency of the state legislature to assure greater access by residents wishing to be heard. It was easy for the Board to decide to get involved in anti-discrimination campaigns and work to change the way legislators interacted with constituents because Virginia Organizing's structure was set up to tackle these issues head on. The harshness of the new Voter ID laws also led to the most recent incarnation of the Martinsville/Henry County Chapter. People came together to voice their opposition, and after that campaign ended, decided to keep working together on other issues.

## ORGANIZING ON SOCIAL SECURITY

In 2011, there was enough traction and interest among leaders to begin a Social Security strategy committee at Virginia Organizing. That summer, Virginia Organizing sent teams of interns and community leaders statewide to make hundreds of community presentations on the current state of Social Security. State Governing Board Treasurer Jay Johnson explained the issue well. "As a senior, I know for a fact that there is a lot of misinformation out there about Social Security. So, one day, Virginia Organizing said enough is enough. We need to set the record straight for seniors and young people alike."

The leaders and interns made a total of 96 Social Security presentations in South Hampton Roads, Richmond, Fredericksburg, Prince William County, Southside and Southwest Virginia at senior centers, places of worship, nursing homes, and community centers. They debunked myths about Social Security and shared ways to take action to protect the program for future generations, including getting about 1,000 postcards from constituents to Senator Mark Warner. This was an effort in education because the political advertisements and media stories surrounding Social Security were confusing and tended to be politically charged: they were designed to get votes and viewers, not distribute facts. Virginia Organizing presented accurate, non-partisan information so that seniors and others could be fully informed and form options for clear next steps to take. Social Security is far from secure because politicians threaten cuts to the program regularly, but Virginia Organizing remains committed to efforts that would strengthen and protect Social Security and those who benefit from it.

Virginia Organizing garners the attention of prominent politicians by holding constituent meetings with U.S. Senators and members of Congress, encouraging people to write about their experiences in letters to the editor or op-ed pieces, and making sure that constituents are consistently communicating the need to protect and strengthen Social Security to those who are in power to do so. Sometimes, Virginia Organizing has done this in connection with other state or national groups, but mostly, the organization has worked within the statewide strategy committee to develop ideas and create plans for local Chapters. This is one example of how an existing organization with a strategic plan in place can play a defensive role and respond to attempts to cut an important program.

## ORGANIZING ON IMMIGRATION REFORM

Although Virginia Organizing had worked with other organizations that had a Latino/a base for many years, Virginia Organizing's platform did not intentionally expand to include issues specific to many Latino/a people until 2010 when the Chapters in the Shenandoah Valley became aware of and concerned about issues around immigration. Organizers and leaders held dozens of one-to-one conversations throughout the community. Areas with a high concentration of Latino/a residents were targeted for door-to-door canvassing. In addition, part of the strategy for the Chapters in the early stages of working on immigration reform was raising awareness that there was a problem with our immigration system and that underlying racism was at the heart of the issue. Chapters held documentary screening events of the film 9500 Liberty, the story of a grassroots movement in Prince William County, Virginia, that led to the repeal of a controversial law allowing police to question those who appeared to be immigrants.

In 2012, the Shenandoah Valley Chapters worked with other groups on a listening project. Chapter leaders discovered that immigrants in the Valley did not feel safe reporting crimes to police officers and that two-thirds of the people interviewed knew someone who had been deported. From the listening project, a report was produced that found undocumented immigrants were being deported for low-level offenses, such as minor traffic violations and other civil and non-violent crimes. Traditionally, the policy of the United States had been to focus on more serious offenses or violent crimes to be considered for deportation, so this represented a change. From an economic standpoint, deportation for a minor civil infraction does not make sense. It costs money to detain people and transport them to another country. But Virginia Organizing believed that it is also immoral and unjust to separate families because of resident "status."

Because of the work of the local leaders, in conjunction with other groups, in questioning why local officials were detaining undocumented immigrants for unrelated charges, Rockingham County elected officials began to seriously reconsider an arrangement that the local Sheriff's office had with the federal government that deputized local law enforcement as Immigration and Customs Enforcement (ICE)

Harrisonburg Chapter leader Jossimar Diaz-Castro attended a town hall meeting for his U.S. Representative, House Judiciary Committee Chair Bob Goodlatte. Diaz-Castro asked Representative Goodlatte about his position on immigration reform and challenged the Congressman on his refusal to allow a comprehensive immigration reform bill passed by the Senate to come to a vote in his committee.

agents. After reviewing the report on the program, known as 287(g), the Rockingham County Board of Supervisors terminated the partnership. This is another good example of how Virginia Organizing leaders participated in a national campaign in support of immigration reform in a local way.

The Chapters in the Shenandoah Valley continued their work for immigration reform by holding multiple rallies where hundreds of people showed up in support of national comprehensive immigration reform with a path to citizenship for the 11 million undocumented immigrants living and working the United States. The U.S. Representative for the Valley, Bob Goodlatte, was the chair of the House Judiciary Committee, which oversees immigration reform bills. Because of Virginia Organizing's work on the issue, Representative Goodlatte heard stories from young undocumented people who had come to the United States as children (known as DREAMers or DREAM Activists, a term that originally took its name from the DREAM Act – short for Development, Relief and Education for Alien Minors Act. The DREAM Act would have granted legal status to certain undocumented immigrants who were brought to the United States as children, grew up in the U.S. and went to school here.) He also answered questions from immigrant constituents about his position on immigration reform and was pushed to identify his position to people in his district. Although Representative Goodlatte did not take action, directly affected people were able to raise their voices and be involved in a national campaign. Virginia Organizing received widespread national media attention for the immigration reform work, which encouraged leaders to keep raising their voices for change.

After many years of Congress failing to provide a solution for immigrant families, President Obama announced in 2012 that his administration would use prosecutorial discretion and stop deporting young people and those with low-level or non-violent offenses. The new program, Deferred Action for Childhood Arrivals (DACA), allowed immigrant youth to live, be educated, and work in the U.S. without fear of deportation. Virginia Organizing leaders and people across the United States called the White House to encourage President Obama to take action and expand DACA. In 2014, President Obama expanded DACA to include more immigrant youth and the parents of American citizen children. This program was called DAPA or Deferred Action for Parents of Americans.

Virginia Organizing South Hampton Roads Chapter leaders gathered on the first day of each month for 24 months to vigil in support of comprehensive immigration reform with a clear path to citizenship.

Virginia Organizing leaders and Board members spoke out about the President's actions but always tried to focus on the more permanent solution of comprehensive immigration reform with a path to citizenship in general. After the DAPA announcement, Board Chairperson Sandra A. Cook said in a media release, "The President's announcement means that the undocumented parents of certain citizen and legal permanent residents will be able to live without fear of being ripped apart from their children through deportation. While Virginia Organizing is excited that President Obama is using the Constitutional powers of his office to protect families, this action does not change the fact that Congress needs to work together and enact bipartisan, comprehensive immigration reform with a clear path to citizenship for our immigrant neighbors."

Chapter leaders have also raised their voices and taken action on immigration reform throughout the process. Speaking at the same DAPA announcement, South Hampton Roads Chapter leader Linda Peña, whose mother qualified for DAPA, said, "Let's be clear: this is relief, not reform. We appreciate relief, but we need reform that is comprehensive and inclusive of all undocumented immigrants living in the U.S."

Virginia Organizing remained committed to lifting the voices of and organizing directly affected people, especially on national issues like immigration reform. Dulce Elias, a young Harrisonburg Chapter leader, frequently participated in actions in her district and held conversations with Representative Bob Goodlatte, her Congressman, about DACA and comprehensive reform. "As a DACA recipient, it is important to me that we stay involved and focused on immigration reform, as this issue affects so many people in our community," said Elias.

Harrisonburg Chapter leader Stan Maclin helped provide the economic reasons behind responsible, comprehensive immigration reform: "There are multiple studies showing how beneficial comprehensive immigration reform with a path to citizenship will be on the U.S. economy," he said. "A path to citizenship will increase revenue, add jobs to the economy, and prevent a decrease in our gross domestic product."

Virginia Organizing remained committed to reform, but also realized that the obstacle of convincing Congressional leaders to move forward was too great to overcome at this time. Throughout the course of the fight for comprehensive immigration reform, new people have become involved in Virginia Organizing and the organization has expanded to hire bilingual organizers where this makes the most sense. In the South Hampton Roads

Chapter, monthly vigils were held to "Light the Way" to immigration reform. The Chapter earned a victory with this campaign by convincing their U.S. Representative, Scott Rigell, to write a letter to House leadership asking that they move forward with immigration reform.

Because of Virginia Organizing's work on the ACA and other issues, leaders from the organization were invited to the White House six times in 2012 and a few times in 2013 to honor that work, attend briefings and meetings, and participate in media conferences. Small business leader Toan Nguyen (pictured, fourth from left), owner of C'ville Coffee in Charlottesville, was invited to the White House in July 2013 as part of a Virginia Organizing delegation and stood directly behind President Barack Obama as he discussed the benefits of the Affordable Care Act for small business owners. Nguyen was invited to meet President Obama prior to the media conference. "It was wonderful to be invited to the White House to support the Affordable Care Act," said Nguyen. "This law supports my small business and I'm glad to return the favor."

## ESCALATING ON MEDICAID EXPANSION

Virginia Organizing Chapters organized on Medicaid expansion both state-wide and locally in 2014. In one action that targeted Speaker of the House of Delegates Bill Howell, leaders rallied and marched to his office to deliver a homemade coffin symbolizing the number of people that were expected to die that year due to lack of health insurance. A media release from this action had several different perspectives on Medicaid expansion:

Eunice Haigler is a Virginia Organizing Fredericksburg Chapter leader and one of the Virginians who would benefit from Medicaid expansion.

She spoke at the vigil on Sunday.

"I was always told Virginia is for lovers, but where is the love for me?" said Haigler. "Medicaid expansion would help me get life-changing treatments for chronic conditions and would bring jobs to Virginia. I wish Speaker Howell would stop thinking about his own feelings toward the Affordable Care Act and Medicaid and start thinking about the 400,000 Virginians who need coverage and are being denied that coverage by the Speaker. Mr. Speaker, please hear the voices of your constituents: we need health care now."

Well-known community leaders joined Haigler, including former Mayor of Fredericksburg Reverend Lawrence Davies.

"Medicaid expansion is a moral issue that has been overly politicized," said Davies. "This is about how humans relate to each other. Those who are unable to receive health care services for whatever reason are still part of the human 'chain' and still belong in our communities. We are already paying for Medicaid expansion to make sure that those who need services the most are being covered, why would we think it's ok to leave our fellow humans out in the cold without health care? This program is not a handout, it's a hand up to proactively get basic health care needs satisfied."

Dr. Patrick Neustatter, medical director of a free clinic and Virginia Organizing supporter, believes expanding Medicaid in Virginia is the reasonable and right thing to do.

"As a doctor and medical director of a free clinic, I see so many people who are uninsured or have lost their insurance, who are sick through bad luck, not because of something they have done wrong. People just get sick," said Neustatter. "In a wealthy society, we should be able to care for these people who otherwise finish up made destitute by their illness. There are compelling moral and medical reasons to expand Medicaid. And it makes financial sense as it allows preventive care and keeps people out of emergency rooms. If only legislators would just see sense, put aside political ideology, stop trying to follow their own agenda, and instead do what's best for Virginia."

Brian Johns and Ellen Ryan wrote an article for *Social Policy* for the Winter 2013 edition, "Leadership Development is Not a Deliverable." An excerpt from their article discusses the deep organizing that was happening in the Shenandoah Valley:

> It's time to shift the focus … onto leadership development and community organizing that reaches the scale needed to make major change *and* build powerful community organizations. This approach works, many community organizations in addition to Virginia Organizing have been doing it for years, and it can continue to expand in communities all over the country. Simply repeating the Health Care for America Now strategy over and over again without taking a breath to build and expand the capacity of community-based organizations to develop committed leaders is shortsighted. Here's an example of how deliberate community organizing and national campaigns fit together.
>
> In 2010, the organizer who covered Virginia Organizing's work in the northern Shenandoah Valley left to take another position. The board and leaders had been planning to do additional strategic work in Spanish-speaking communities and used this opportunity to hire a bilingual organizer to spend the next several *years* having one-to- one conversations with Spanish-speaking people, many of whom work in the poultry industry throughout the Valley. All she did for an entire year was one-to-one meetings with people from all across the Valley to find out what issues were important to them. Based on these conversations, a local chapter organized and chose its own issue: to address racial profiling in the Latino community by local law enforcement. The chapter began work to end the local enforcement arrangement the Sheriff had with federal immigration officials.
>
> Because the organizer had met with members from across the community, it was possible to build relationships between African-Americans and Latinos early on through meetings between members from each community. Chapter members learned dozens of skills, including

writing letters to the editor, organizing meetings, speaking in public, presenting grassroots education on the issue, doing a power analysis, developing a campaign strategy, and meeting with elected officials. After two years of work, the chapter won the campaign and, just as importantly, had organized an intentionally diverse chapter of directly affected community members who worked to dismantle racism, learn new skills, and alter the existing power relationships in the Valley. Very little of this work was supported by national campaign funding.

As the chapter was working to decide on its next campaign, the national immigration reform issue once again took center stage. Virginia Organizing became the lead organization for the Alliance for Citizenship, leading the organizing in eight of Virginia's eleven Congressional districts. One of those districts is in the Shenandoah Valley and represented by Congressman Bob Goodlatte, who chairs a key House Committee on immigration issues. The Valley chapters and members were able to turn out 400 members to an immigration rally in April and followed that up with hundreds of members putting pressure on Representative Goodlatte for months. And yes, there has been a great deal of media coverage. The level of engagement and widespread support for immigration reform in this key district would not have been possible without the years of investment in local organizing and leadership development. Members had learned skills and developed relationships as a group, and could influence decision-makers on any issue that might come up.

This is just one example of community organizing providing reach and power to national campaigns. Virginia Organizing was able to do similar work during the HCAN campaign, covering districts and pressuring members of Congress all over the state, all while doing leadership development and building the organization.

## SHARING ORGANIZING LESSONS WITH YOUNG PEOPLE

While Chapters were working on immigration issues affecting their constituencies, they were also hosting outside groups, such as students from the University of Massachusetts who have visited annually since 2010 during their spring break to learn about organizing and participate in canvassing and other community outreach activities. Students were also welcomed from the College of William and Mary. The student groups were able to see the complexity of working in support of national and statewide campaigns while maintaining a commitment to local leaders. Chapter leaders learned about new technology, organizing and social change theories being taught in the classroom, and what issues were important to college students from the young people. Virginia Organizing has been able to balance these goals by analyzing power at all levels of decision-making and working to build the local Chapters and leaders within those Chapters.

Organizers and other staff are often asked to share their expertise in classrooms or other settings with groups. Not only have Virginia Organizing staff shared their community organizing and non-profit experience with groups at the statewide and national levels, but they have on numerous occasions sent staff abroad and received guests from other countries for various learning opportunities. Chapter members were able to learn from students, interns, and fellows what issues were important to them, what tactics are being used in organizing in different settings, and how organizing is done in other places. Interns and other Chapter visitors added to the diversity of voices in the group, offered different perspectives, and helped generate new ideas for the future.

"Working with young people through internships and classes helps to plow the ground for the future," said State Governing Board Debra Grant. "They may be the community leaders and maybe even community organizers of the next generations."

CHAPTER 10

# Keeping the Vision

**AFTER ALL THE VALIANT** legislative efforts for Social Security protection, immigration reform, Medicaid expansion, protection of voting rights, increased transparency in state politics and redistricting, and more on the statewide and national levels from 2009 to 2013, there was a shift in 2014. The State Governing Board decided Virginia Organizing should strategically refocus on building local Chapter capacity, help leaders develop new skills and sharpen existing ones, and equip Chapters to work on non-legislative and local campaigns. Legislative campaigns, those that focused on a policy change through enactment of law, were simply not working in Virginia or at the federal level because of political logjams. The political climate in 2014 and 2015 was hostile to families and supportive of corporate, big money interests. Nationally, the political calculus of elected officials outweighed respecting the democratic process and the best interests of the United States as a whole. Because of a small group of people in extremely powerful positions, legislative change was elusive, and resources needed to be redirected to achievable goals, building power in Chapters, and achieving wins at the local level. In community organizing, wins and celebrations are an important part of strategic development and growth. The Board understood that legislative campaigns would likely frustrate directly affected people and dampen enthusiasm for change. The state and national political climate was not going to allow for economic, social, and environmental justice, so Virginia Organizing went back to some basic power analysis questions to make organizing at the local level more effective: what do we want and who can give it to us?

Through a comprehensive power analysis, the Board identified four key areas that were ripe for change using local and non-legislative campaign strategies: criminal justice, predatory lending, immigration (local focus), and voting rights/civic engagement. To allow a greater number of people to participate in this process, task forces made up of local Chapter leaders and Board members were created to organize these campaigns. This resulted in Chapters working more on specified local campaigns that would change the lives of people in their communities. Virginia Organizing maintained a commitment to national issues like immigration reform and state issues like Medicaid expansion and health care reform, but shifted more energy to the local Chapters and local campaigns and non-legislative work. One of those campaigns was to ban the criminal history application question (an effort often called "ban the box") on public job applications in different localities.

## VIRGINIA NEEDS MORE GRASSROOTS ORGANIZING

Virginia Organizing had made a commitment to refocus on local organizing after the Power Analysis Weekend in April 2014. This decision was affirmed when, as part of a 2015 power analysis of organizations working for social change in Virginia, Amy Cohen, a veteran community organizer, shared an overview about the need for more grassroots organizing in the Commonwealth.

Cohen wrote, "Some groups directly acknowledge having a focus other than organizing. But more claim to do a kind of organizing and speak about a 'base' while explaining away the need to work directly with people and create spaces for affected individuals to be a part of the organizations and campaigns they are building. A majority of groups profiled develop and maintain their 'base' almost exclusively through online contact... When these are the building blocks of organizations' 'grassroots efforts', and the rest of their work happens between and amongst staff and elected representatives and other traditional power brokers, these strategies only serve to reinforce the stratification that already exists in communities and across the Commonwealth. Changing this dynamic requires a different approach."

Cohen also concluded that the lack of grassroots community organizing in Virginia was "to the detriment of the aim of achieving long-term sustainable changes." The analysis affirmed Virginia Organizing's approach to organizing in Virginia as necessary for involving directly affected people in changing and challenging traditional power structures, while maintaining many opportunities to take action at the local level. The report also highlighted the need for more base-building grassroots organizing in the state.

Grassroots community organizing that is inclusive of people who are directly affected is about more than changing laws and policies, it is about changing people's lives through leadership development and personal growth.

## BAN THE BOX

Many Chapters decided to push their local governments to ban the box throughout Virginia. The "box" represents the checkbox beside a question on most job applications about whether or not the applicant has ever been convicted of a felony. It is usually used by employers to screen out this population and exclude them from consideration, regardless of other qualifications.

Many employers will say that criminal history is not a disqualifier when considering which applicants are invited to interview, but research suggests otherwise. A study published in Volume 57, Number 4 of *The Journal of Correctional Education* in 2006, "Where Do Ex-Offenders Find Jobs? An Industrial Profile of the Employers of Ex-Offenders in Virginia" by Eric Lichtenberger, showed that only 8.2 percent of employers in Virginia had employed a former offender from 1999-2003, meaning more than 91 percent of the employers in the state had not hired anyone with a criminal record, even though many contend that they would. Virginia Organizing believes that disqualifying a person from employment because of a past mistake is a form of oppression that keeps people from being full participants in our society, much like the denial of the right to vote until the Governor restores their civil rights. The box itself creates a barrier: if employers say they are willing to hire someone with a criminal record, Virginia Organizing believes that they should take the box off the application and let a person's qualifications speak for their ability to do the job. (Of course criminal records checks can happen later, but only after the applicant has a chance to be considered.) Ban the box campaigns have happened in various places around the U.S.

Thanks to Virginia Organizing Chapters, sometimes in collaboration with other groups, the box was removed in Charlottesville, Danville, Fredericksburg, Martinsville, Newport News, Norfolk, Portsmouth, and Virginia Beach.

"Virginia Organizing seeks to assist citizens returning from incarceration in the process of being a part of their community," said Virginia Organizing State Governing Board member Duane Edwards. "Virginia Organizing has found that the ban-the-box campaigns give individuals a better chance to obtain employment."

Virginia Organizing leaders and other groups also asked the Governor to ban the box on state job applications and these efforts paid off! Wins in many localities provided a solid foundation and contributed to a supportive environment for an executive order from Virginia Governor Terry McAuliffe to remove that criminal history question from state job applications. In March 2015, when Governor McAuliffe announced this statewide ban, Virginia Organizing leaders were there to celebrate with him and thank him. In addition, after Virginia Organizing met with the chiefs of staff of U.S. Senators Mark Warner and Tim Kaine on criminal justice matters and many people encouraged them to take action, the Senators signed on with 24 other U.S. Senators to a letter to President Barack Obama asking for executive action to ban the box on federal job applications.

Karen Shaffer and Barbara Williamson rallied at the Washington County Board of Supervisors meeting in 2014, calling on their elected officials to fight against hydrofracking. Shaffer has been involved in organizing against hydrofracking for years because of her concern about its effect on the environment, particularly land and water use. In a 2011 Virginia Organizing newsletter, Shaffer was quoted as saying, "I believe the future holds safer ways of harnessing energy, and thoughtless drilling today will only lead to regret tomorrow. The natural gas 'bridge' leads to nowhere – we all need to see beyond the money." Washington County residents were disappointed that their elected officials ultimately decided to allow hydrofracking, but they continued to organize and began testing water supplies to create a baseline measurement for quality before hydrofracking began.

This is a great example of a non-legislative campaign that still used organizing tactics of storytelling, phone calls, letters, conversations with elected officials, and public actions. The campaign required that constituents form relationships with either their town or city council members to make the decision locally, or on the statewide level, with the governor and members of his administration. The campaigns were not always easy, but building relationships with elected officials is a skill that leaders of this campaign, most of whom had been incarcerated, were excited to learn. A person with a criminal record who has served time for a felony – who has been taught that his or her voice does not matter – talking to elected officials is an example of what Virginia Organizing is all about. Real people are creating real change by raising their own voices and finding confidence and power in the process. That is leadership development.

## OTHER NON-LEGISLATIVE CAMPAIGNS

Another example of non-legislative work was focusing on civic engagement in unique ways, such as hosting block parties in areas of town with low voter turnout and including restoration of civil rights applications and educational materials in addition to voter registration applications at these events. "It is important to make sure all people who are eligible to vote in Virginia are registered and understand why they need to vote," said Harrisonburg Chapter leader Ricardo Cortez. "Voting is a fundamental right in our society. It is an opportunity for every voice to be equally heard. Virginia Organizing wants to make sure that every eligible voter has the chance to raise his or her voice."

Other action and campaign ideas generated by task forces and local Chapters included petitioning localities to impose restrictions on predatory lending like payday and car title loan companies, working with local law enforcement on immigration issues to ensure the civil rights of undocumented immigrants are protected, and working on criminal justice issues by interrupting the school-to-prison cycle in Virginia school districts. Some of these campaign ideas are still in the planning stages and others are in progress. Each Chapter works on its own local campaign in addition to building power on non-legislative ones.

Chapters also continued to understand justice issues in a micro and macro way. One example of this is environmental justice. In a macro sense, climate change, pollution, and water quality affect every single person on the planet; at a micro level, these things also have very real local consequences for specific people. One key example of this is the threat of hydraulic fracturing or "hydrofracking" in Washington County. For more than four years, Virginia Organizing fought against the natural gas industry's plan to extract the natural resource from Washington County and kept them from drilling. However, in 2014, the gas companies won and the Board of Supervisors voted to allow hydrofracking. The process itself is risky and environmentalists have raised concerns of air, water, and soil pollution as well as earthquakes. The local (micro) effect of hydrofracking has the potential to hurt people through water and soil contamination that may threaten water and food supplies or cause physical harm if ingested, cause property damage, and decimate farming land in the County. Virginia Organizing leaders could have given in to defeat and moved on to a new campaign, but the Chapter leaders and the community members are committed to protecting their environmental assets. They chose to get training to learn how to test water for contaminants and to start testing before the natural gas extraction process began. This process provides a baseline measurement of their environment, which could make proving contamination of natural resources easier in the future. This is an organizing tactic as well as a service. Although one avenue in the local campaign was lost, Virginia Organizing helped local residents take control of their situation and work on other strategies to protect their health, property, and future.

## PERSISTENCE AND LONGEVITY COUNT: ORGANIZING AROUND RACIAL PROFILING

In 2002 and 2003, as leaders and staff were doing hundreds of one-to-one conversations across the state, there was a recurring theme as people of color frequently talked about being stopped, detained, frisked, or generally targeted due to race. Around that time, North Carolina state police began collecting data on traffic stops and then analyzing it. As a result, VOP decided to organize a racial profiling campaign with the initial goal of getting the Virginia General Assembly to pass legislation requiring data collection on traffic stops. After years of only doing local organizing, and building on the momentum from the first successful statewide affordable housing campaign, this became VOP's first state legislative campaign.

VOP organized a group of leaders from around the state to develop a strategy. Building on the past work of state Senator Henry Marsh, newly-elected state Delegate Jeion Ward agreed to introduce a bill. Leaders and staff then spent months identifying directly affected people to speak to the Virginia House of Delegates subcommittee that would hear the bill. The subcommittee consisted of six white men, none of whom had VOP Chapters in their districts. Instead of allowing leaders to testify, the chairman of the subcommittee, former Rockingham County sheriff Glen Weatherholtz, quickly called for a motion and a second to "pass the bill by indefinitely," effectively killing the legislation. Within moments, VOP's first attempt to push for state legislation was over before it really got started. After the hearing, on the street corner outside of the Virginia General Assembly Building, VOP leaders got a chance to evaluate the campaign and came to a clear conclusion: we did not have the power we needed at that time and we would need to increase our efforts in a big way.

Over the course of the next several years, the racial profiling campaign took many twists and turns. There were meetings with the Virginia State Police Superintendent and the Executive Directors of the statewide law enforcement organizations. The Superintendent attended a VOP annual meeting in Richmond with more than 100 members in attendance.

In November 2003, VOP was pleased when then-Governor Mark Warner announced that there would be standards for police training and policy models aimed at eliminating racial profiling, including a policy change that would make it easier for citizens to report incidents of racial profiling. Still, nobody at the state level agreed to do data collection.

At that point, like at many points in the organization's history, leaders decided to re-strategize and not focus on the state level. During the next several years, new Chapters were organized and several of them focused on racial profiling in one way or another. While there was not enough power to win the issue legislatively or administratively, Virginia Organizing was building relationships and organizing directly affected people all over the Commonwealth.

Because of the organizing in localities around the state, by 2014, Virginia Organizing was in a very good position to build on local responses to police brutality nationally, and to support or take the lead in organizing people on the issue in their own communities. Chapter leaders had meetings with several local police chiefs, who made commitments to collect data in order to better serve communities of color in their own jurisdictions. Some of the chiefs agreed to persuade their colleagues in other localities to do the same. This work continues as more Chapters hold more meetings with more police chiefs.

Virginia Organizing's work on racial profiling is an excellent example of how building power over the long haul and organizing a broader web of relationships across the state can fail, adapt, and succeed because more leaders are constantly identified and developed to carry on the work.

## VOTING RIGHTS

Virginia Organizing is committed to working for change right where people are. While the organization believes elections are important, it is also important to work to hold elected officials accountable through constituent contact, not just at the polls. As a non-partisan organization, Virginia Organizing continuously emphasizes voter registration and access to voting. In 2013, access to the polls was limited by legislation requiring non-photo voter identification. Prior to the 2014 elections, legislation passed restricting voter access further by requiring voters to show photo identification at the polls. Virginia Organizing and other groups who had spoken out against this change in legislation for years went right to work, making sure that people knew about the change and knew they could get a photo ID card from the State Board of Elections (now the Department of Elections), while emphasizing voter registration as much as they had in prior years. Virginia Organizing encouraged local registrars to actively get qualifying IDs to people who did not have them and assisted with the restoration of voting rights for people who could not register.

These types of actions around civic engagement keep local leaders involved in their community and help Virginia Organizing reach new people who can potentially become a part of the organization and work to create change. Registering and educating voters in a non-partisan way is a great example of an ongoing non-legislative campaign that empowers individuals to use their voices and gives Chapter leaders an opportunity to connect to more people through the process. It is a strategic plan that accomplishes multiple goals:

Virginia Organizing leaders gathered in 2013 with the NAACP, AARP, and other groups to protest the requirement of photo identification at the polls. Photo ID laws are a barrier to the constitutional right to vote and can be used to prevent lawfully registered individuals from exercising that right. Because of Virginia's history of participation in Jim Crow, any hindrance to voting should be taken seriously. Moreover, instances of voter fraud are so minute that they are statistically insignificant, yet Virginia and other states have spent millions of dollars implementing voter and photo ID laws to intimidate and prevent people of color and other traditionally marginalized groups from casting their ballots. Denise Smith and her granddaughters were at the rally, where Denise spoke about the importance of protecting access to the polls for all people.

leadership development, civic engagement, recruitment, and building more capacity for power within the organization.

In 2014, Virginia Organizing leaders, including two State Governing Board members, were arrested outside of U.S. House of Representatives Speaker John Boehner's Washington, D.C. office. Virginia Organizing Treasurer Jay Johnson shared this about her experience: "All my life I worked to avoid arrest and here I was volunteering to get arrested to support our immigrant brothers and sisters in the fight for comprehensive immigration reform."

Eunice Haigler of Fredericksburg never dreamed she would be risking arrest in solidarity with youth Latino/as. She got active in Virginia Organizing because of criminal justice issues and voting rights and also became interested in health care issues. When she heard the stories of young immigrants in her community, she was moved to take action and volun-

Kate Rosenfield and Alicia Bobulinski were led from Speaker of the U.S. House of Representatives John Boehner's office after being arrested for standing with immigrant youth in support of comprehensive immigration reform.

teered to risk arrest at Speaker Boehner's office. "I was prepared for the handcuffs, prepared for the processing, but I was not prepared of how I would feel once the door to the cell shut," said Haigler. "I knew the outcome of my arrest, but it hit me that there were thousands of immigrants out there being detained for deportation who do not know their fate. They are taken from their homes to a cell filled with uncertainty. That was hard."

All Virginia Organizing leaders were released, but their bold action still resonates with local leaders today. Although there was an emphasis on local actions, this opportunity for leadership development was a good example of using different organizing tactics within a campaign – including civil disobedience. Virginia Organizing had built strategic organizing capacity that could be used in a national campaign. Virginia Organizing spent a year deliberately doing leadership development to lead up to this action!

Over the course of 20 years of organizing in Virginia, sometimes things did not work so well.

Some Chapters ran out of steam because we did not build a solid foundation.

Some leaders were interested in solving a local problem, but not in building an organization with a long-term approach. Some leaders cared a lot about an issue that was important in their life, but didn't want to work on other issues that were important to their neighbors and other Chapter members.

Some campaigns failed: some were too ambitious, sometimes we misread the political landscape. Sometimes we just got beat because we hadn't built enough power to change a system.

Some organizers and apprentices were not good fits at Virginia Organizing. We learned that we had to invest a great deal of time and energy in new organizers and have realistic expectations for their first few years on the job while they learned the ropes and developed their skills.

We tried some grassroots fundraising strategies that just didn't work: Indiegogo, Kickstarter, some time-intensive events turned out not to be good methods for the organization.

In some cases, we tried to do too much and did not meet our goals. It's easy to forget that even with a dedicated staff and an organization full of committed leaders, there are still only 24 hours in a day.

There were times when we got frustrated with some of our partners and decided to stop investing time and energy in those relationships. These are difficult judgment calls. For example, we invested heavily in large-scale canvassing and phone banking operations, but eventually realized that they did not support leadership development and growth of local Chapters. National and statewide elections became distractions instead of organizational enhancements and funding for those campaigns had narrowly-focused interests that did not allow us to pursue the sort of dynamic, adaptable organizing models which laid the foundation of Virginia Organizing.

We needed to be honest about the effectiveness of working with other groups. Too many decisions in coalitions were haphazard and not based on a sound power analysis. In addition, some other statewide groups that we had hoped would develop stronger and longer-term organizing plans chose different paths to move forward.

There were times when we acted too fast, other times when we moved too slowly. It took us a long time to figure out that we needed our own internal communications coordinator, for example. Lots of groups across the country had established communications departments before we began to invest in that capacity at Virginia Organizing.

Sometimes we tried to participate in a national issue campaign, but found that it didn't make sense without a clear plan and a target that included long-term organizational building components.

We continually work to improve our leadership trainings and materials, especially with regards to racism, heterosexism, and the economy. We learned – and relearned – that people need to build relationships and share their experiences, that leaders want to make change and also to feel connected to other leaders. It meant we had to take our time and make space for relationships to grow, even when that meant slowing down the timeline for a campaign.

Virginia Organizing leaders have always been willing to experiment and were willing to discontinue programs or campaigns when they no longer made sense. As a learning organization, Virginia Organizing has been able to navigate through missteps, setbacks, and failures. Growth and expansion are seen as imperative, year after year. Power analyses, strategy charts, and constant evaluation have contributed to a positive approach of "keeping the energy moving forward."

Virginia Organizing's commitment to intentionally debriefing both successes and failures, to learning lessons together without assigning blame, to challenging one another to make decisions that both feel good and are strategically sound help make sure we can get up when we stumble, dust ourselves off, and keep moving forward on the road toward many more years of success.

– Joe Szakos

# CHAPTER 11

# Future Expectations

**VIRGINIA ORGANIZING** has always implemented a strategic planning process to ensure that every single action, issue, and event has a purpose that aligns with the Organizing Plan adopted annually by the State Governing Board. The organization is visionary and truly believes that the world can always be more just for more people and that to get to an ideal of justice, we need to keep building power together. There have been many different ways this has occurred, as shown throughout this book. At this pivotal time in the history of Virginia Organizing, the organization has honed in on this focus.

In October 2015, the staff has grown to 20 people, with 13 community organizers. The Board has set a goal of eventually having 20 community organizers across the state and has set aspirational and attainable fundraising goals. A part of achieving these goals was a new practice: having each Chapter responsible for fundraising at least $5,000 annually. Setting this expectation allows Chapter leaders another opportunity to connect to the larger picture of the statewide organization, gives them a new set of skills to learn and master, and creates a stronger connection to the unique focus on grassroots donations that allow Virginia Organizing to continue the work.

Chapters are not just a part of the organization; they set the agenda and invest in their own capacity to create change. Leaders get to learn more about what it takes to build and sustain an organization like Virginia Organizing and have more incentive to be a part of supporting the organization through their own financial contributions or in-kind donations. This allows Virginia Organizing to do real community organizing!

The Board and staff work hard to ensure leaders are not only equipped to work on their local issues but that they understand what is going on with other Chapters around the state. There are lots of ways they do this: through social media and the Virginia Organizing website; regular newsletters; encouraging attendance at the annual Grassroots Gathering; providing "good news of the day" updates to key leaders, Board members, and all staff that are shared in meetings; and e-mail blasts to encourage action and provide updates.

## THE GRASSROOTS GATHERING

At the annual Grassroots Gathering, leaders learn new perspectives on issues and organizing tactics, which is even more helpful if they are feeling stuck in a campaign. The Grassroots Gathering is the annual meeting of Virginia Organizing, where Chapter leaders help tie together all the work done over the year, and in recent years has become a way for leaders to be involved in direct action.

At the 2012 Grassroots Gathering, Virginia Organizing members boarded three buses and went to Anthem CEO C. Burke King's house to present him with a thank-you card and balloons for giving Virginia Organizing a refund for overpayment of premiums (a requirement of insurance companies after the ACA became law).

At the 2013 Grassroots Gathering, Virginia Organizing hosted State Board of Elections representative Garry Ellis to discuss voting rights and access in the state, along with Governor Bob McDonnell's Secretary of the Commonwealth Janet Vestal Kelly to talk about changing the restoration of voting rights process.

Lieutenant Governor Ralph Northam and Secretary of the Commonwealth Levar Stoney attended the 2014 Grassroots Gathering. Virginia Organizing leaders from communities across the state were able to ask Lieutenant Governor Northam a host of questions in a mass meeting about children's issues, criminal justice, Medicaid expansion, and more. In a separate session, leaders got a commitment from Secretary Stoney to meet to determine ways to further streamline the process for the restoration of voting rights for those with a felony conviction.

These conversations with people in positions of power gave Virginia Organizing leaders a chance to make demands for change and build relationships to facilitate that change. Overall, these activities increase the grassroots force of the whole organization because connections are made across geographical lines, consistent with Virginia Organizing's commitment to diversity at all levels.

## LASTING CHANGE THAT MAKES A DIFFERENCE

As Virginia Organizing celebrates its 20th anniversary in 2015, the organization is making statewide connections in new and exciting ways. Every month there have been celebratory events throughout the state, including a salsa dancing night in Fredericksburg, a benefit concert in Charlottesville, a Green Walk to kick off a new local campaign in Petersburg, a potluck meal in Wytheville, and more. Many Chapters successfully petitioned their local governments to issue resolutions in honor of Virginia Organizing's 20th anniversary; these proclamations line the walls of the Charlottesville office to help celebrate all that has been achieved. U.S. Senator Mark Warner read a statement into the *Congressional Record* congratulating Virginia Organizing on 20 years of grassroots organizing and the Virginia General Assembly passed a commending resolution during its 2015 session.

Davon Miller received his certificate restoring his voting rights in a meeting with Virginia Governor Terry McAuliffe and Secretary of the Commonwealth Levar Stoney, just before the Governor's Restoration of Rights Media Conference in December 2014.

Real change is a slow process. The founding Organizing Committee knew that back in 1995 and the State Governing Board knows it now. Virginia Organizing has created lasting change that makes a difference in the lives of real people.

In Roanoke, people who identify as transgender are getting better health care because Virginia Organizing leaders, including directly affected people, met with hospital administrators to ask for change.

In Albemarle County and Charlottesville, public schools have anti-discrimination policies that include LGBTQ staff and students because Virginia Organizing helped students and teachers organize for change.

In Harrisonburg, as in all of Virginia, the state Attorney General has declared that individuals with an Immigration and Customs Enforcement (ICE) hold on their records for immigration status can no longer be detained without cause. Virginia Organizing leaders met with local sheriffs across Virginia to find out their positions on ICE holds and urged them to stop honoring these holds because the organization believed they were a violation of the U.S. Constitution. (Virginia Organizing members had made hundreds of calls to the Attorney General's office and had a meeting in November 2014 asking him to issue the opinion. Those meetings and calls made a difference.)

Across Virginia, people with felony records are registered to vote or have received their voting rights because for more than 10 years, Virginia Organizing stepped in to empower and engage individuals through one-to-one meetings, community events, and local restoration of rights clinics and then worked with them to change the system.

In several communities across the Commonwealth, police chiefs are collecting data on racial profiling to ensure that all people are treated fairly and with respect.

In 2015, organizers are building new Chapters in Roanoke, Lynchburg, Newport News, and the New River Valley, while existing Chapters in Charlottesville/Albemarle, Danville, Fredericksburg, Harrisonburg/Rockingham County, Lee County, Martinsville/Henry County, Petersburg/Tri-Cities, Richmond, South Hampton Roads, Staunton/Augusta/Waynesboro, and Washington County continue to work on local and wider issues.

New local campaigns are being developed as the needs of the communities change and evolve.

Over the last 20 years, Virginia Organizing leaders made a difference in their communities every single day. The next 20 years and beyond will give Virginia Organizing leaders even more opportunities to build power and change lives.

This is another excerpt from Brian Johns' and Ellen Ryan's article in the Winter 2013 edition of *Social Policy*, "Leadership Development is Not a Deliverable".

Naming a bridge to honor a local Native-American tribe, passing local ordinances against payday lending and in support of living wages, getting toxic chemicals removed from neighborhoods, stopping racial profiling by law enforcement, and restoring the rights of many former felons to vote are just a few of the successful campaigns defined and carried out by local people working together over long periods of time. The issues local groups choose to work on can be anything people in the community decide is important to work on. The point is that the issues provide a means for people to learn together how to use the power they have to plan and take effective public action as a group.

In addition to addressing a wide range of local issues, Virginia Organizing has worked deliberately to build a multi-issue, member-controlled power base with the capacity and scale to link local chapters together to work on broader issues and form coalitions with other groups when needed. Local leaders from all parts of the organization meet to discuss broader issues that chapters can't effectively address alone and select issues for research and training that leads to organization-wide campaigns and coalition building with other groups interested in working on them.

The first organizing plan...focused on rural communities like Lee County in the southwest Cumberland mountains and Wytheville, nestled in the Blue Ridge, intentionally avoiding the densely populated Richmond and northern Virginia areas where numerous local and policy-focused groups already existed. The staff and board had no preconceived campaign agenda. Instead, the local chapters were built systematically through hundreds of face-to-face conversations and small meetings with local residents, gradually building public relationships and group research on possible solutions to local issues identified by members.

Racism, long an obstacle to building multi-racial groups in the South, was addressed head-on in the organizing plan and through hundreds of dismantling racism workshops over the years that brought people together to talk about how racism damages and distorts their ability to get things done together.

Later Virginia Organizing chapters formed in other parts of the state, including Lynchburg, Petersburg...Charlottesville, Harrisonburg, Danville, Fredericksburg, and Hampton Roads...

This was an "outside-in" strategy, a purposeful effort to begin to build an organization slowly and carefully, away from the Richmond-centric thinking that everything important that happens is a policy initiative at the state house. Local members learned together how to plan and chair chapter meetings, talk to the local media, raise money, deliberate with public officials, take stock of the progress the group made, and plan the next steps. Members learned whom they could trust, how power operated in the community, and who among them was best suited to various leadership roles in the group.

# Accomplishments

**VIRGINIA ORGANIZING** (formerly the Virginia Organizing Project, or "VOP") accomplished a lot over the past 20 years. This chronological list includes many, but not all, of those accomplishments.

One thing we are proudest of is that diversity is at the core of everything we do and will do. We are committed to helping people who have never been active before to raise their voices and join with others who have already tackled community problems, enabling them to organize together, regardless of race, gender, class, sexual orientation, occupation, geographic location, or ability. To do so, we have developed sound training programs dealing with dismantling racism, economics education, building public relationships, and other leadership skills. Virginia Organizing has become a successful model for Virginians to see how different constituencies can organize – and win – together. We continue to effectively move people to action to create a more just Virginia!

## 1995-1998

* The VOP Chapter in Lee County successfully challenged the jury selection process used in the county at the time, claiming the process was not fair to people of color. As a result of the campaign, for the first time ever, an African-American was appointed as a jury commissioner. The county then changed the selection process for the jury "pool" by moving to a random selection process, instead of the previous system in which five white men chose their friends for the jury pool, a process that had eliminated all people of color and most low-income residents. This was our first local victory!

* Working with other community groups, labor unions, and community development corporations, with strong support from the Financial Markets Center, VOP helped to push the Federal Reserve Bank of Richmond to set up a formal mechanism to deal with issues of concern to low-income and working class people,

known as the Community Development Advisory Council. This was a major institutional change to the way the Federal Reserve Bank of Richmond operates.

* VOP sponsored Dismantling Racism workshops throughout the state beginning in 1995. In some cases, it was the first time that such a workshop was held in that locality. Several organizations made major changes in the way that they operate as a result of these workshops. Among the groups that held a Dismantling Racism workshop were the Richmond Peace Education Center, Virginians for Justice, Equality Virginia, NARAL Virginia, United Methodist Women's Conference (Blackstone), Virginia Sexual and Domestic Violence Action Alliance, Burnley-Moran Elementary School faculty (Charlottesville), Jefferson Theatre-BBTV, and the YMCA of the Virginia Peninsula. We also held Dismantling Racism workshops on the following campuses: Christopher Newport University, University of Mary Washington, College of William and Mary, Virginia State University, University of Richmond, and Emory and Henry College; we also held a workshop for the senior classes at Petersburg High School.

Besides making the Dismantling Racism workshops available to groups and communities in Virginia, we conducted workshops for the Appalachian Community Fund, Save Our Cumberland Mountains (Tennessee), and the (national) Sierra Club for its East Coast staff. VOP presented a workshop on how Dismantling Racism helps to build a strong people's' organization for a conference of the National Coalition of Education Activists, "Reclaiming Our Children's Future: Uniting Families, Schools and Communities."

Community groups started to have a better understanding of racism and began challenging hiring practices of public agencies, the lack of diversity in the school curriculum, and issues concerning law enforcement. Dismantling Racism workshops led to the Town of Wytheville providing a host of infrastructure improvements (sidewalks, water/sewage, and road paving) in predominantly African-American neighborhoods and the first African-American principal at a high school in Wythe County. In Washington County, workshop participants went to work and got their local school board to adopt a "zero tolerance racial harassment" policy. Workshop participants in other areas worked on racial profiling, living wage, "ban the box," and restoration of voting rights campaigns as a result of what they learned.

Specific examples of the wider effects of these trainings include a Lee County school psychologist who presented a paper on dismantling racism and white privilege to all county guidance counselors, and a publisher of the local paper in Wythe County who changed the way it covered race issues and ran editorials that reflected a major change in perspective.

In addition to holding workshops for leaders and members, VOP staff attended a wide range of trainings to be better prepared to facilitate trainings, as well as to incorporate more of the Latino/a experience into our Dismantling Racism workshops.

---

*From 1995 through 2014, Virginia Organizing held 32 three-day and 67 one-day Dismantling Racism workshops with a total of 2,381 participants — in Abingdon, Accomack County, Alexandria, Amherst County, Arlington, Charlottesville, Colonial Heights, Danville, Emory, Emporia, Fairfax, Fredericksburg, Hampton, Harrisonburg, Jamestown, Jonesville, Kilmarnock, Lovingston, Lynchburg, Marion, Martinsville, Newport News, Northampton, Norton, Pennington Gap, Petersburg, Richmond, Virginia Beach, Waynesboro, Winchester, Wise County, Woodstock, and Wytheville.*

---

* Prior to VOP's organizing, there were few options for a new and emerging local grassroots organization in terms of leadership training and consulting on organizational development. VOP has held trainings on leadership and democratic skills, sexual orientation issues, and the nuts and bolts of community organizing, along with a wide range of political education workshops on economic, environmental, and social justice issues. Workshops included a training on op-ed writing by Barbara Ehrenreich and Helena Cobban; a Principles of Community Organizing class at the University of Virginia in conjunction with the Carter Woodson Institute for African and African-American Studies; a training event on computer-based strategic research led by Will Collette of the AFL-CIO Research Department; and, a roundtable discussion on economic issues with journalist Bill Greider. VOP also led a workshop on *Engaging New Constituencies and New Voices* at the National River Rally sponsored by the River Network and a workshop on *Organizing for the Long Haul* at the Institute of Management and Community Development in Montreal, Quebec.

*From 1995 through 2014, Virginia Organizing held 1,660 workshops and trained more than 36,400 individuals. Many monthly Chapter meetings include a training component to help local people build leadership and organizing skills.*

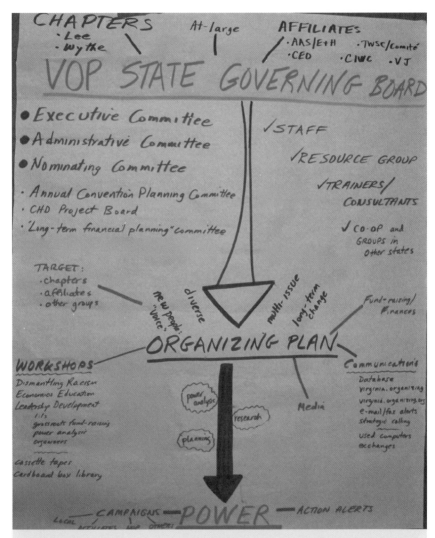

The VOP State Governing Board was very deliberate and intentional about developing a clear plan for how the organization would operate. This newsprint is from a meeting in 1998.

* Many local groups fought to stop a power line in the western part of the state. VOP worked with them to make some broader issue connections and co-sponsored a forum on utility deregulation in Wytheville.

* With the statewide organizing support that VOP was able to give, corporations that were originally refusing to pay benefits resolved two workers' compensation cases in Martinsville. During these campaigns, many people learned that it is important to do corporate campaigns and that it helps to flood a government agency with letters, calls, and faxes while such an administrative process is underway.

* VOP began work on many living wage campaigns, including the northern Virginia living wage campaign, and the campaign at the University of Virginia.

* VOP developed some powerful tools that would prove to be helpful for community organizations – local and statewide – to be more effective, including an e-mail action alert system, a quarterly news magazine, a used computer project, and numerous leadership materials.

---

*By early 2015, the e-mail action alert system grew to 9,280 subscribers.*

---

* VOP started sending out a newsletter in December 1995. In January 1998, the publication turned into a 32-page quarterly news magazine, *virginia.organizing*, with a circulation of more than 6,500, that provided news of VOP and its Chapters, gave news of other groups in the state, and had sections on organizing skills (in English and Spanish) like "Win and Build the Power of Your Organization" and "Elements of Strategy: Constituents, Allies and Opponents" and "Tips for Chairing Meetings." We ran articles on out-of-state waste, chip mills, dismantling racism, sexual orientation, living wage, free speech, homelessness, the death penalty, and a host of other social justice issues. We also had a section on "Understanding the Economy" in each issue; articles included: "Tultex a Virginia Victim of Free Trade" and "Virginia Rides the New Economy" and "Virginia Wages: Are We All Better Off?" and "Virginia Taxes Punish the Working Poor." Later, we added a new feature article, VOP Leadership Profile, with stories about key VOP leaders. The last issue of the quarterly news magazine format was Fall/Winter 2007, when the worker-owned printing cooperative

that we were using went out of business. We then shifted to an electronic format and now send out a regular two-page newsletter – still including a leadership profile!

*From our inception, we have had a priority of increasing grassroots fundraising each year. Besides asking individuals for donations, we have held house parties and brown bag lunches, sold ads for program books for our annual meeting, had a sliding scale for registration fees for workshops, solicited donations from faith communities, accepted payroll deductions (including the state employee Combined Virginia Campaign), sent out three direct mail appeals each year, collected used cell phones and printer cartridges, and had a wide range of Chapter fundraisers – from yard sales to benefit concerts to Latin dancing nights to adult Easter Egg hunts. We also have major gifts and planned giving programs. All organizers and leaders learn how to raise funds for the organization so that everyone is invested in the success of Virginia Organizing.*

*Also, we started a phone banking fundraising program in 2013 that has increased the number of individual donations we receive. We are working on a more integrated online fundraising approach. We also are promoting EFT (electronic fund transfers) and other monthly sustainers so that we can create a steady stream of donations from the broadest group of people.*

*Virginia Organizing accepts grants and donations for about 40 other groups and handles their payroll and bookkeeping functions for a fee. Income generated from this service covered all of our administrative costs (administrative staff, insurance, audit, occupancy, etc.) in 2014.*

*We drive donated cars (17 of them). We get lots of donated or bartered office supplies and equipment. From 1999-2014, we received more than $255,000 in in-kind donations (not counting the cars): furniture, office supplies, office maintenance, and repairs. To say we are frugal would be an understatement. This means that we can say to donors and funders, "All the money we receive from you will go directly into moving people to action!"*

* VOP actively worked on welfare reform with the Campaign for Virginians in Need, including helping to organize a rally of 450 people at the state capitol in February 1995.

* As a result of putting a longer-term focus on our work, and holding lots of Dismantling Racism workshops, the VOP State Governing Board formed an ad hoc committee to develop plans for Dismantling Heterosexism, Sexism, and Classism workshops and decided to work on a package of economic/tax reform measures that required a broad political education training program.

* We learned that it is possible to develop a pool of "home grown" facilitators (leaders and staff) for Dismantling Racism workshops. By having our own "team," we are able to do the necessary prep work and follow up directly with the participants. In the past, other groups had told us that workshops were not integrated into their overall program as much as needed, and this approach addressed that need.

* We were able to develop new avenues to involve students in social change work and started an internship program.

*From 1997 through 2014, we have had 510 interns, with internships ranging from a few months to two years. Some received academic credit, some were paid, and the vast majority were Virginians. Interns also came from Bulgaria, Germany, Hungary, Romania, and Slovakia. In addition, Virginia Organizing participated in international exchange programs on civic participation with individuals from Afghanistan, Bangladesh, Mexico, and Sierra Leone.*

* VOP was able to develop a diversified funding base through grants, donations, and in-kind contributions. Many in-kind donations were made to VOP for our office building in Charlottesville (purchased in 1998): a $3,000 phone system, free installation of the phone system, paint, sheetrock, carpeting, electrical supplies, a copier, and a truckload of office furniture – all coming from new sources. In addition, major renovation work to the building was done mostly by volunteer carpenters, electricians, and plumbers, as well as dozens of other individuals. Besides offices for our staff, we are able to provide offices for other non-profits and a meeting space for community groups.

# 1999

* VOP had a major growth spurt during this year and added three staff people – a lead organizer, another community organizer, and a development director – and David Rubinstein became VOP's General Counsel. VOP also provided financial support for the Tenants' and Workers' Support Committee to add an organizer in northern Virginia to organize Latino/Latina-led local community groups.

* VOP submitted substantial comments on payday loans to the Federal Reserve Bank in support of stronger regulations.

* We held two one-day test workshops on exploring heterosexism and then held one full session on sexual orientation issues.

* VOP supported Virginia Forest Watch's efforts to oppose chip mills planned for Dickenson County and helped convince the legislature to pass a bill to study the impact of satellite chip mills on the economy and environment and another study of existing timbering practices to ensure streams and rivers were being protected.

* State legislation putting harsh restrictions on TANF (public assistance) was defeated because VOP worked with others groups to get hundreds of phone calls to legislators.

* The Fund for the Virginia Organizing Project, Inc. was established as VOP's Endowment.

---

*From 1998 through 2014, the endowment was able to provide $174,499 to the operating budget of Virginia Organizing, plus funding four new energy-efficient cars. The value of the endowment as of December 31, 2014 was $1.5 million.*

---

* We hosted a Hungarian environmentalist, Gabor Prtiskz, in conjunction with the Southern Empowerment Project. This was the first of many exchanges with organizers from other states and countries, including some long-term exchanges. VOP leaders and staff also visited other countries to share their experience with community organizing.

* At the request of VOP, the Charlottesville City Council passed a resolution to encourage the legislature to adopt language to include sexual orientation in the hate crimes law.

* VOP facilitated the long-term planning process for the Richmond Peace Education Center. This was one of many ways in which VOP provided leader and staff support to other organizations on strategic planning, organizational capacity building, and leadership development. VOP focuses on encouraging local groups to grow in numbers, participation, and power by intentionally crossing barriers and building meaningful public relationships in their communities.

*From 1999 through the end of 2014, Virginia Organizing provided 1,628 consultations to groups in Virginia on campaign strategy or organizational development. Our belief is that we all benefit when we work with other groups to help them enhance their capacity to make change happen.*

* Several Chapters worked on Martin Luther King, Jr. Day celebrations and race unity days, and met with local governments and school officials on anti-discrimination policies.

* We helped the Montebello Clean Mountain Coalition in their campaign to successfully get the Central Virginia Electric Cooperative to refrain from spraying pesticides on a landowner's property.

* Four cars were donated this year, starting the practice of having the organization provide each organizer with a vehicle. This helped reduce operating costs, especially with many mechanics providing donated or reduced-cost services.

*From 1999 through the end of 2014, Virginia Organizing received 65 donated vehicles. Those that were not needed for organizers were sold at auction or given away.*

* The Charlottesville Branch of the NAACP gave VOP an award for outstanding support of their organization.

*From 2003 through the end of 2013, VOP leaders and members had more than 165 op-eds and 615 letters to the editor published and were interviewed by radio and TV reporters on more than 130 occasions, and "Virginia Organizing" appeared in the print media more than 1,330 times.*

*In 2014, our visibility continued to grow and we had a wide range of actions and forums and distributed 81 media releases that resulted in 292 media "hits". In addition, in 2014, VOP leaders had 142 letters to the editor published.*

\* We hosted a tour of community/economic development projects for officials of the Federal Reserve Bank of Richmond on the Eastern Shore and in Louisa County.

## 2000

\* VOP and its affiliates worked on successful living wage campaigns in Alexandria and Charlottesville, increasing wages for hundreds of low-wage workers. These victories encouraged people in other localities to begin living wage campaigns in their communities. The Labor Action Group (LAG) and other groups at the University of Virginia were successful in pushing the university to pay its workers at least $8.46 an hour, a major increase at the time. (VOP did several strategy sessions with LAG leaders.) Continued pressure resulted in the Charlottesville City School Board and the Albemarle County School Board raising wages for their lowest paid employees.

\* We successfully challenged the Alexandria Housing and Redevelopment Authority to issue its notices in English and Spanish.

\* A VOP affiliate, the Montebello Clean Mountain Coalition, succeeded (working with other groups) to get 10,000 acres in Nelson County designated as federal wilderness area.

\* Led by four student interns, VOP succeeded in a campaign to convince the Charlottesville School Board to add sexual orientation to its non-discrimination policy for students and employees. An intergenerational strategy team brought together a wide range of constituency groups to push for the policy change.

* We continued to work on Federal Reserve Bank issues as we took Richmond Federal Reserve Bank President Al Broaddus on a tour of Latina/o communities in northern Virginia. Various Fed publications still reflect some of the lessons learned from these tours.

* The Wythe County Chapter met with the Community Affairs Office at the Richmond Federal Reserve Bank, who agreed to hold a "Making Small Towns and Cities Work" conference in Wythe County with VOP and the Wythe County Chamber of Commerce, the first of its kind by the Fed in a rural area in Virginia.

* Student interns for VOP began compiling a list of Charlottesville employers who pay a living wage. It became obvious that the hotel industry was paying sub-par wages, so VOP targeted Courtyard by Marriott: protests outside the Charlottesville Courtyard by Marriott occurred every Friday for 107 straight weeks, resulting in the Mayor working with local hotel operators and Piedmont Virginia Community College to link job training with increased wages.

* We began to work hard to develop ways for more people who got active in VOP to understand the economy. We held workshops on "Getting the Economy to Work for All of Us" at our annual meeting and had briefings from national experts on living wage campaigns and on taxation and revenue issues in the state.

* VOP developed a good working relationship with the Financial Markets Center, a non-profit organization that provides research, information, and analysis on financial markets, the Federal Reserve System, and the impact of their policies, as well as several college professors who made presentations focusing on local economic security issues, as we tried to make connections to broader economic issues.

* VOP has always provided the staff with opportunities for growth leave and ways to "stretch" themselves. VOP also has a tradition to send all new staff organizers to Midwest Academy's five-day organizing training. All staff gets five days of "growth leave" each year to pursue training to strengthen their skills.

* With the assistance of VOP's attorney, we revamped the memorandum of under-standing with the groups for which we accept grants and donations, as well as the employment contracts related to these groups. Eventually, we developed

a Joint Plan of Work program that gives each group more time and resources to work on their social justice and environmental missions, while Virginia Organizing provides bookkeeping, payroll, insurance, and auditing services.

* VOP developed a more comprehensive and strategic media plan to increase our visibility.

## 2001

* VOP successfully worked with a broad-based coalition of groups to urge state legislators to block legislation that would have prohibited localities from enacting living wage ordinances.

* We made a presentation to the Annual Conference of the United Methodist Church in Virginia, which adopted a resolution supporting the living wage.

* After more than five years of focusing on local organizing, we officially kicked off our first statewide affordable housing campaign, which resulted in the Virginia Housing Development Authority making the following significant policy changes:

Maggie Murphy was instrumental in building and cultivating Virginia Organizing's fundraising phone bank program. She has coordinated benefit concerts for Virginia Organizing – and for programs in Darfur and Sudan. The sign held by the boys in the photo reads, "Thank You Maggie Murphy for your generous commitment and friendship with Ariang School."

⁓ VHDA opened its doors to all legally documented immigrants (formerly, only immigrants with permanent resident status qualified for VHDA loans).

⁓ The VHDA Board created a $45 million loan program, called SPARC, to provide homeownership loans to people who do not qualify for other VHDA loans at a 5.5 percent interest rate. (VHDA rates were 6.8 percent.)

⁓ The VHDA Board approved adding a Section 8 resident to its Board.

✓ Also, VHDA:

- enacted changes in the Low-Income Housing Tax Credit program that require developers to provide relocation money to tenants displaced by rehabilitation projects financed with Low-Income Housing Tax Credits;
- improved public access to the VHDA Board after we began sending observers to the Board meetings;
- added a public comment period to the beginning of the full Board meetings and announced that they were willing to meet with groups for 30 minutes prior to the Board meetings;
- voted to re-open the issue of discrimination against unrelated adults, a policy that allowed them to refuse to make loans to gay couples and other unrelated people attempting to become homeowners (this resulted in a public hearing on January 3, 2002, and eventually led to a major change in policy);
- received suggestions from their consultants that VHDA could still meet its "depression scenario" tests by projecting its activity for one year rather than the current five years, and make an annual decision on how to allocate funds at the end of each fiscal year.

* The VHDA Board later voted to make about $400 million in funds available for low- and moderate-income housing in the state.

* We worked with Chapter members in Lee County to get the local schools to continue offering Advanced Placement classes and found four teachers who agreed to become certified.

* We continued to send out major action alerts via our e-mail network. One of the alerts, combined with the efforts of our affiliate, Virginians for Justice, prompted a church in northern Virginia to cancel a "cultural war training" promoted as a session to "help defeat the forces that are trying to push homosexual rights in Virginia."

* The Lynchburg Chapter successfully organized to change the long-term suspension policy in the city schools so that students receive appropriate alternative education and counseling rather than a mandatory 365-day suspension.

* VOP initiated a project with the Virginia Commonwealth University Video Arts

program to document the history of the Bayview community on the Eastern Shore and produce the video documentary "The Black Soil".

* VOP partnered with the 4-H Youth Development Program of Northampton County Extension to hold diversity conversations with high school students.

* VOP worked with a group of students, teachers, and community members to successfully get sexual orientation added to the non-discrimination policy in the Albemarle County schools.

* We supported the efforts of the Richmond Coalition for a Living Wage as they got the Richmond School Board to pay its workers a living wage. We also provided training support for living wage campaigns at six colleges and universities.

* VOP co-sponsored Days of Dialogue (on Race Relations) in Charlottesville and entered into partnership with public TV station WHRO's initiative on race through Colors All Our Own. WHRO serves the eastern part of the state.

* VOP met with leaders from the NAACP, ACLU, Virginia CURE, and other organizations to begin planning for more serious work around racial profiling and restoring voting rights for former felons; this became a new statewide campaign for VOP in 2002.

## 2002

* VOP played a critical role in encouraging Virginia's governor to make major changes to the voting rights restoration process. Governor Mark Warner agreed to reduce the application form from 13 pages to one page for former non-violent felons, replaced the five- to seven-year waiting period with a three-year waiting period, and promised that applicants would receive a response within six months of submitting an application where, previously, no time limit for a response had been set.

* The Amherst Chapter studied its school system's suspension policy for racial bias and determined the county was implementing the process fairly.

* While actively involved in the campaign for restoration of voting rights to former felons, the Lee and Wise County Chapters held a community training

event on assisting former felons through the restoration application process. This event raised the awareness of the Virginia Organizing Project and saw an increase in participation and interest.

---

*From 2002 through the end of 2014, Virginia Organizing held more than 140 clinics and trainings around the state on restoration of voting rights.*

---

* The Lynchburg Chapter organized to push the Lynchburg City Council to remove racist artwork from public properties. The bas-relief at the Circuit Court building was particularly offensive, as it depicted black slaves with faces like chimpanzees. Such artwork could only intimidate and denigrate Lynchburg area residents who come trusting in the objectivity of the court system. The Chapter succeeded in having this artwork removed. The public reaction to this change was very positive and brought the support of other community organizations. As a result of the increased community support, another offensive depiction in the Juvenile and Domestic Relations Court building was completely covered by an American flag.

* Citizens for a Better Eastern Shore, Nature Conservancy, and the 4-H clubs of Northampton and Accomack partnered with the Virginia Organizing Project to sponsor a day camp for preteens to talk about diversity on the Eastern Shore.

* The Wythe County Chapter held an awards ceremony dedicated to recognizing local businesses that pay a living wage. As a result of this event, VOP attracted the attention of other employers in Wytheville.

* During this year, VOP adopted a comprehensive staff growth plan, added the capacity to do GIS mapping, upgraded all our technological systems (including e-mail and database), and upgraded and expanded our website.

## 2003

* Our state tax reform campaign celebrated two successes in 2003: $7 million was generated by closing the foreign royalties income loophole and $211 million was saved by stopping the repeal of estate taxes on estates over $1 million. We held 41 "Who Pays and Who Benefits?" workshops throughout the state during the year.

* Our media presence grew significantly in 2003. We were featured in articles in the *Washington Post*, the *Richmond Times-Dispatch*, the *Virginian-Pilot*, and the *Roanoke Times*, to name a few. We were credited in a variety of publications in Virginia with providing continued grassroots leadership in addressing tax reform.

* VOP successfully worked with Equality Virginia to realize the completion of another objective in our affordable housing campaign. In July 2003, VHDA removed a rule that barred unrelated couples from applying for loans. This policy had been used to discriminate against gays and lesbians.

---

*From 2003 through the end of 2014, Virginia Organizing had 882 constituent meetings with state legislators and Members of Congress to discuss issues of importance.*

---

* The Amherst County VOP Chapter organized to have a new bridge over the James River named the "Monacan Bridge" to recognize the local heritage of the Monacan People, the indigenous people of central and western Virginia.

* The Lee County Chapter organized a candidates forum for the fall elections which was essential in a vote that overturned the local power structure that refused to address racial and economic justice issues of critical concern to the community.

* The Lynchburg VOP Chapter worked to get a safety barrier put on a bridge that was a high-risk location for suicide attempts.

* Virginia Organizing Project's annual meeting highlighted the need to address police racial profiling. Members of VOP directed questions and shared stories and concerns with Col. W. Gerald Massengill, Superintendent of the Virginia State Police. Members pushed for his support regarding data collection on all traffic stops and to have the data analyzed by an independent agency to identify any racial bias.

* The Petersburg VOP Chapter met with various city officials, which led to the city filling a vacant position for a fair housing officer/housing ombudsman, a position that had not been filled for five years.

* Leaders and members from many VOP Chapters met with their state legislators to discuss inequities in the state tax system.

* VOP received a generous donation to fund a comprehensive remodeling of the first floor offices at 703 Concord Avenue in Charlottesville to provide complete handicap accessibility.

## 2004

* In 2004, VOP joined the Virginia Alliance for Worker Justice, a new partnership of religious, community, and worker organizations, brought together to promote an increase in the Virginia minimum wage from $5.15 to $6.50 an hour. In this campaign, VOP worked with the Virginia Council of Churches, the Virginia Muslim Coalition, the Catholic Diocese of Richmond, and other groups.

* The Charlottesville City Council passed a budget resolution linking the living wage to the cost of living index, ensuring a continual rise in wages at the lowest tier. In our work with students at the University of Virginia, a contracted service provider for the University, Aramark, increased wages for its dining hall workers.

* VOP coordinated a living wage workshop for students from nine Virginia college campuses. Guest speakers included Ben McKean from United Students Against Sweatshops and Barbara Ehrenreich, author of *Nickel and Dimed: On (Not) Getting By In America*. In addition, VOP provided assistance to living wage campaigns in Richmond, Lynchburg, Blacksburg/ Montgomery County, the Wythe County School Board, and Emory and Henry College.

* During the 2004 election year, VOP's work included non-partisan voter registration and mobilization activities around the state. In the spring, VOP published a voter's guide for the Charlottesville City Council races. The 16-page guide included information about the general election for City Council, how to register to vote, where to vote, and how to vote by absentee ballot.

* Working with the Center for Community Change, VOP worked to increase civic participation in the national electoral process. VOP published *No Vote, No Voice*, a non-partisan voter education guide, and distributed 90,000 copies statewide through 118 organizations and adult literacy programs. We produced and distributed public service announcements to 276 radio stations statewide.

* VOP received an award for "dedicated services" from the Virginia Coalition for the Homeless.

* Virginia State University students took a public stand on racial profiling by holding a media conference in Petersburg.

* VOP's high school and summer interns worked on an accessibility project, studying public facilities in their community to determine what the needs are for wheelchair accessibility. This initial research helped the Independence Resource Center to develop a local guide regarding accessibility for their constituents.

* From 2004 through 2012, we held an annual fundraising event in Charlottesville, the Social Justice Bowl. Virginia potters donated handcrafted bowls; restaurants, caterers, and individuals donated soup, and bakeries donated bread. Annually, a crowd of VOP

VOP held a voter rights conversation at Norfolk State University for students and community members.

supporters each chose a bowl, filled it with soup, and enjoyed a great evening in which we honored some of VOP's stalwart volunteers.

* VOP continued to receive recognition for our fundraising efforts. In 2004, we answered requests from other organizations interested in building stronger grassroots fundraising programs. Some organizations that received fundraising consultations included: Appalachian Sustainable Development, Neighborhood Resource Center in Richmond, RAIL Solution, Shelter for Help in Emergency, Virginians for Alternatives to the Death Penalty, and the Virginia Minority Supplier Development Council.

# 2005

* More people were able to improve their campaign strategy skills through the expansion of more Chapters and implementation of strategy teams for statewide issue campaigns, which allowed for a powerful combination of directly affected people working with issue experts on power analysis, strategy and campaign planning, and implementation.

* Following up on VOP's successful statewide distribution of a non-partisan voters' guide in 2004, VOP distributed a non-partisan voters' guide for the 2005 state-wide elections as well.

* We did a project in conjunction with Environmental Health Sciences and worked with Finger Lake Productions to produce a series of 60-second radio programs with the series title *Envirominute*, to be broadcast on the radio nationally five times per week for a year.

* VOP supported Equality Virginia in its successful effort to pass legislation to allow private employers to offer health insurance and other benefits to domestic partners.

* VOP members came to the Virginia Holocaust Museum to speak out against racial profiling and support efforts to get the Virginia State Police to collect racial data on traffic stops.

* VOP provided major consulting support to JustChildren, a legal aid group working on children's issues, to pass a statewide policy to require the Virginia Department of Juvenile Justice to develop regulations that provide mental health service transition plans for incarcerated juveniles with mental health needs prior to their re-entry into the community.

* VOP worked with the Independence Resource Center to do a survey of each school in Charlottesville in terms of accessibility. As a result of the surveys, the city maintenance department made many improvements to the schools, while longer-term projects were added to the capital improvements budget.

* Concerned with racial profiling issues, local and developing Chapters held face-to-face constituent meetings with more than 40 state legislators, as well as

meetings with local sheriffs and chiefs of police in at least nine communities and discussions with the staff of the Department of Criminal Justice Services and the Chair of the Virginia Crime Commission.

* VOP expanded its relationships with Muslim and Latin American organizations. The president of the Virginia Muslim Coalition and other Muslim leaders served as key speakers at VOP's racial profiling rally in Richmond and new Latino organizations participated in organizing Chapters in the Shenandoah Valley.

The 2005 annual meeting provided VOP leaders with opportunities to learn more about building power, leadership, and democratic skills

## 2006

* VOP distributed petitions and collected signatures for an increase in the minimum wage at numerous public events around the state, gathering more than 35,000 signatures in 2006.

* At the request of VOP, Delegate Jeion Ward submitted legislation to address racial profiling that would have mandated simple data collection on all traffic stops by all law enforcement.

* In April, 17 students were arrested at the University of Virginia during a peaceful sit-in organized to support a living wage for all university workers. Several VOP interns co-led this effort, which galvanized the community around the disparity

between the prosperity of the University and the relative poverty of many of the workers the University depends upon.

\* VOP held the VOP Leadership Institute, with a dozen participants from Hampton Roads, the Peninsula, Richmond/Petersburg region, Shenandoah Valley, and southwest Virginia. Participants got together for four weekends of intensive training during the year.

\* The Williamsburg VOP Chapter was involved in an affordable housing campaign to make their community a place where those working in the area can afford to live. They organized a housing forum that outlined the strengths of inclusionary zoning to raise public awareness and recruit new participants. At their second public forum on affordable housing, there were 50 attendees, suggesting that interest in affordable housing was growing in Williamsburg and James City County.

VOP helped organize an immigrant rights rally in Richmond in April 2006.

\* The Roanoke Valley VOP Chapter joined with the Roanoke NAACP and the local Alumnae Chapter of Delta Sigma Theta Sorority, Inc. to sponsor a City Council Candidates' Forum at William Fleming High School.

* We had eight people testify (four mental health consumers) at the Virginia Housing Development Authority's public hearing about affordable housing.

* VOP worked with other groups to release a report on the achievement gap in the Charlottesville City Schools.

---

*Besides the initial power analysis when VOP started, we have conducted an annual power analysis starting in 2006. We did this in many forms over the years, but the focus remains constant: who has power in Virginia and who does not? By answering these questions, we can determine how we can seriously affect change in Virginia. The State Governing Board incorporates what we have learned from the annual "Power Analysis Weekend" (held at the end of April) into the annual Organizing Plan.*

---

* VOP co-sponsored a forum with Public Policy Virginia and other groups called "Biofuels: For Our Environment, Economy and Security."

* We helped to organize and sponsor a rally to support immigrant rights in Richmond's Monroe Park, which more than 3,000 people attended.

* VOP helped to coordinate a town hall meeting in Norfolk on the future of the media, with more than 300 people attending and 77 speaking.

## 2007

* VOP held 24 forums on poverty, mental health, and predatory lending.

* We worked with other groups to push for passage of a state tax reform bill that removed approximately 150,000 low-wage workers from the Virginia tax rolls and prevented almost 150,000 more from having to file tax returns to get their refund of withheld taxes. We were successful in getting a raise in the filing threshold from $5,000 to $7,000 for individuals and from $8,000 to $14,000 for married couples, plus an increase in the personal exemption from $800 to $900.

* VOP pushed for state Senate passage of a minimum wage increase and, for the first time, the Virginia House Commerce and Labor Committee reported the

minimum wage increase out of committee to the floor of the House of Delegates. Unfortunately, the bill was killed by an unusual procedural vote on the House floor that sent the bill to a committee that would not be meeting again during the session.

* Virginia Organizing Project mourned the loss of minimum wage legislation by holding a public funeral procession from 5th and Broad Streets in Richmond to the State Capitol.

* We continued a campaign concerning racial profiling, pushing for funding for data collection by law enforcement officers in Virginia. While the campaign was not successful, it laid the groundwork for later efforts of our Chapters to get commitments (in 2015) from several police chiefs to begin to collect data at the local level.

* Working with several other groups in the Verified Voting Coalition, VOP supported passage of a bill prohibiting future purchases of direct recording electronic voting machines, phasing them out and replacing them with optical scan voting machines which provide a paper ballot, giving the voter confidence in the accuracy and security of elections.

* VOP worked with an emerging coalition, Virginia Partnership to Encourage Responsible Lending (VaPERL), to bring payday lending industry practices into the spotlight and set the stage for a push for a major initiative in the 2008 General Assembly session. As part of that campaign, the Central Shenandoah Valley VOP Chapter sponsored a public meeting featuring a credit counselor and a former payday lending operation manager talking about alternatives to payday loans; a Northern Virginia Strategy Committee was set up to prepare for predatory lending campaigns in Fairfax and Prince William Counties; working with local leaders and interns, VOP recruited exploited payday lending consumers to tell their stories on local Roanoke Valley radio and raised awareness of the issue; more than 450 payday lending surveys were completed in Richmond/Petersburg; and the Virginia Beach VOP Chapter pursued local angles on predatory lending, including mapping payday shop locations, speaking before the city's Human Rights Commission, and implementing a "matched savings" empowerment initiative to provide individuals an alternative to predatory lending entrapment.

* Northern Shenandoah Valley VOP Chapter members and allies spoke to six

governing bodies about increasing affordable housing. They also critiqued all five fair housing forums in the region.

* VOP co-sponsored a dozen non-partisan candidate forums across the state for local as well as statewide races.

* In the summer of 2007, VOP conducted an exploratory local campaign, knocking on doors in Virginia House District 58 asking two questions: (1) Do you have an old cell phone or printer cartridge that you would like to recycle? and (2) Do you know that interest rates as high as 390 percent are being charged for payday loans? If the resident expressed concern about the high interest rates, they were encouraged to contact their state legislator to cap the interest rate at 36 percent. This resulted in lots of calls to Delegate Rob Bell's office and led to the creation of a larger canvassing operation the next year.

* We succeeded in getting the Charlottesville City Council to designate $1.1 million to make all school facilities in the city fully compliant with the Americans with Disabilities Act. Charlottesville City Schools became the first school district in Virginia to have all their facilities fully compliant.

* We assisted with a local campaign to keep the Williamsburg/James City County's Alternative School operating. We also assisted with a local campaign in the Williamsburg area around school redistricting, working for racial and economic parity among schools.

* We assisted the Historic Gainsboro Neighborhood group in their victory that blocked the City of Roanoke's plan to build a Social Security Administration office in their neighborhood.

* After interviewing 81 community organizers across the country (while attending national meetings and trainings), Executive Director Joe Szakos and his wife, Kristin Layng Szakos, published *We Make Change: Community Organizers Talk About What They Do – And Why* (Vanderbilt University Press). One of the goals in writing the book was to get more young people interested in community organizing and social change. For a second book project, they recruited a dozen organizers in rural areas to write essays about their experiences, which resulted in *Lessons From The Field: Organizing In Rural Communities*, published by the American Institute for Social Justice/Social Policy in 2008.

* We worked with the Sierra Club to collect hair samples from 30 women at a Portsmouth hair salon; tests showed some levels of mercury in every sample, with two above the EPA "acceptable limit."

*From 2007 through the end of 2014, in addition to phone banking and door-to-door canvassing, Virginia Organizing had more than 10,400 intentional one-to-one conversations with new people (from a wide variety of constituencies) to recruit them for the organization.*

# 2008

* VOP helped get a record 67 local governments to pass resolutions asking the state legislature to take action on the abuses of payday loans, had a visible presence at all of Governor Tim Kaine's town hall meetings across the state, and held direct actions at many payday loan sites; the compromise state legislation resulted in some provisions that work toward breaking the cycle of debt.

* VOP helped organize and initially staffed the Virginia C-3 Table (later changed to the Virginia Civic Engagement Table) so that non-partisan organizations in the state could coordinate their efforts for non-partisan voter registration and get-out-the-vote activities.

* As a member of the Working Families Child Care Coalition, Virginia Organizing supported an increase in funding for childcare subsidies for low-income working families, an increase that was supported by Governor Kaine's administration and approved by the Virginia General Assembly.

* The town of Berryville changed its ordinance after the ACLU threatened to sue on VOP's behalf for being overly restrictive in regulating the right of people to peaceably assemble.

* VOP had a major door-to-door canvass in 2008 during the summer, using 50 paid interns and our organizing staff of eight to knock on more than 140,000 doors, registering voters, distributing a 32-page non-partisan voter guide (which included all the major issues in the state and information about many other organizations), and passing out flyers in key state legislative districts about health care, child care, immigration, and the environment.

* VOP worked with Demos, the Virginia NAACP, Project Vote, and Democracy South to force the Virginia Department of Social Services to make major improvements in its voter registration system to come into compliance with the National Voter Registration Act.

* VOP conducted voter protection training and get-out-the-vote activities, including distributing non-partisan door hangers and voter empowerment cards, phone banking, putting voter information in small business locations and on college campuses, tabling at public events, and giving people rides to the polls – resulting in an increase in voter turnout in the precincts where we focused our efforts.

Clarke County residents held a vigil in 2008 to support fair housing and highlight the need for affordable housing options.

* Fifty VOP staff and leaders attended the Realizing the Promise Forum on Community, Faith and Democracy, a non-partisan event, with members of President-elect Barack Obama's transition team; VOP Chairperson Jay Johnson was a featured speaker at a forum roundtable.

* VOP co-sponsored "Power Up Petersburg" with the Legal Aid Justice Center, Richmond Community Action Program, Gamaliel Foundation, and Local Initiatives Support Corporation to build leadership skills, increase involvement in local community-based initiatives, and encourage a collaborative approach to community work.

* VOP worked with The Commonwealth Institute for Fiscal Analysis to successfully urge legislators to defeat a bill that would have favored large companies with out-of-state business at the expense of smaller establishments.

* Three VOP grassroots leaders attended a media training in New York City with the Center for Community Change to become national spokespeople for the Campaign for Community Values.

* VOP held a meeting, along with four other groups, with the Speaker of the Virginia House of Delegates to outline issues for the 2009 legislative session including health care reform, education, the environment, and the need to pay personal care assistants more.

* We held a wide range of workshops that included a Community Organizing (weekend) workshop with participants from Roanoke, Alexandria, Fairfax, Richmond, Danville, and Charlottesville and a training workshop with a local group in Lebanon, Virginia, working on addiction issues. Our leaders and staff made a variety of presentations and held workshops on community organizing, including to 24 Virginia Community Action agency planners, 13 educators of the Virginia Education Association and at the Annual Conference on Neighborhood Concerns. We spoke to 27 interns at the Phoenix Project on how non-profits work and held a semester-long community organizing training for a class of University of Virginia students titled "Women's Leadership, Feminist Organizing and Social Change."

* We held another VOP Leadership Institute (four weekends) to build a larger network of grassroots leaders across the state.

* VOP sponsored community health care forums in 12 localities to discuss critical health care problems, failings in the system, and possible policy solutions. We helped organize the Virginia portion of the national "Road to American Health Care" bus tour sponsored by SEIU and we recorded video interviews of eight

people telling their health care stories for the Health Rights Organizing Project of the Center for Community Change.

* We implemented a strategy to generate grassroots support to increase health insurance coverage for poor parents (at the state level) and to expand the CHIP program to include more children, including immigrant children (at the federal level).

* VOP leaders worked to get a Drug Court established in Planning District 1 in southwest Virginia. Even though local court officials and local government supported the program, the state legislature refused to fund Drug Courts in the area.

* The Health Care Reform Coalition, of which VOP was an active member, supported Governor Tim Kaine's biennial budget that reflected modest goals; even these efforts achieved only limited success because of a shortfall in state resources due to the effects of the recession.

* VOP worked with Families USA to release six national reports on needed health care reform and to get organizations to sign on to a letter to the McCain and Obama presidential campaigns, encouraging them to make health care a priority.

* VOP held an action outside the Anthem insurance company headquarters in Richmond to press them to become part of the movement for quality, affordable health care for all Virginians.

* We mailed thousands of health care postcards and organized leaders, volunteers, interns, and staff to make thousands of calls to legislators calling for health care reform.

* VOP successfully urged state legislators to defeat a measure that would have given law enforcement officers the unfettered authority to arrest individuals and take them into custody when they were charged with a Class I or II misdemeanor and the measure would have required their arrest if they did not stop the unlawful act.

* VOP joined nine other groups and a Shenandoah County farmer in a federal lawsuit to block plans to widen Interstate 81 to eight or more lanes through much of western Virginia.

* While canvassing door-to-door to register voters in Danville, VOP interns gave out more than 800 free compact fluorescent light bulbs in low-income neighborhoods and helped residents install them to replace incandescent bulbs.

* VOP launched its Facebook page.

*From 2008 through the end of 2014, Virginia Organizing held 532 direct actions and conducted 555 community forums.*

## 2009

* VOP published and distributed 275,000 copies of *Virginia Votes 2009: Your Guide to the Virginia Elections*, a 32-page non-partisan voter guide.

* Since this year involved statewide elections, we hired 40 interns for the summer and they knocked on 155,679 doors in a non-partisan voter registration and get-out-the vote drive. In addition, we made more than 47,000 non-partisan get-out-the vote phone calls.

* VOP was the national Health Care for America Now campaign's lead organization in Virginia. We organized health care forums, rallies, and press conferences with a wide range of groups across the state in which people told their health care stories to legislators and demanded quality, accessible health care for everyone. Virginia Organizing also established a Health Care Reform Strategy Committee.

* VOP sent an action alert e-mail to more than 8,000 people with a toll-free number for help with problems voting and distributed 3,000 non-partisan pamphlets that the ACLU and NAACP produced about voter rights and responsibilities.

* VOP pushed tax reform at the federal level by joining USAction's Fair Tax Campaign to push for an extension of the estate tax, putting together an information sheet on the federal estate tax that included background material, talking points, and action steps, to educate VOP members on the issue.

* We worked with the Institute on Taxation and Economic Policy to release a report showing how low- and middle-income families in Virginia pay a higher

share of their income in state and local taxes than do the richest families in Virginia.

* Virginia Organizing held a protest outside of Anthem's headquarters in Richmond because the company raised the insurance rate for Virginia Organizing employees by 14.2 percent. A small delegation tried to enter the corporate offices during normal business hours to talk to a customer representative during the protest, but Anthem officials locked the main door. Executive Director Joe Szakos was arrested for criminal trespassing when he refused to leave. Virginia Organizing used Szakos' trial as a vehicle to get out the message of how the health insurance industry was unaccountable to its customers. All charges were eventually dismissed.

Jay Johnson spoke at a media conference before the trial of Executive Director Joe Szakos. Szakos was arrested in front of Anthem's Richmond office for criminal trespassing when he and Board members came to ask why the organization's health insurance premiums had risen so steeply.

* At the state level, VOP's Tax Reform Committee used Black Friday, the country's busiest shopping day, to call for reducing or eliminating the regressive state sales tax. VOP's Tax Reform Committee crafted a progressive tax reform proposal that addressed the state's budget crisis, providing for new revenue and keeping vital services from being cut.

* In an effort to support residents raising their voices and participating in the democratic process, Washington County Chapter members successfully pressed the Washington County Board of Supervisors to reinstate a public comment period at its meetings.

* VOP sponsored a forum on Housing in the Northern Shenandoah Valley, attended by more than 80 people, which resulted in local government commitments to improve housing in the area in the coming year.

* Williamsburg Chapter members attended a meeting of the James City County Comprehensive Plan Steering Team, which almost fully incorporated VOP's suggestions regarding mixed cost, inclusionary housing developments for the local workforce.

* The Washington County VOP Chapter and other groups won a local campaign to keep a proposed truck stop from being built at a local exit off Interstate 81.

* VOP organized a delegation of rural Virginians from all over the state who traveled to Washington for a "Rural Issues in Health Care Reform" Congressional briefing.

* VOP volunteers held a series of rush-hour events at their local Falls Church Metro stops to encourage commuters to call Congressman Gerry Connolly and Senator Mark Warner, asking them to support the public health insurance option.

* South Hampton Roads VOP members told their representatives in Congress it is "time to deliver" on health care reform with a series of events that included a canvass day, prayer services focusing on health care reform, a health care reform lobby walk visiting local Congressional district offices, and a Dia de Los Muertos (Day of the Dead) tribute to the 122 people who lose their lives daily due to lack of health insurance.

* VOP joined with the Main Street Alliance for a week of action bringing small businesses together nationwide to advocate for meaningful health care reform. In Richmond, local small business owners rallied together on Main Street, calling attention to the impact skyrocketing health insurance premiums have on their businesses and asking Congress to offer relief.

* Fredericksburg VOP volunteers donning Santa hats gathered outside the Fredericksburg library and asked local residents to sign a "Snowflake Petition" by writing their health care stories and concerns on ornamental snowflakes later delivered to U.S. Senators Mark Warner and Jim Webb.

* VOP members who were unemployed joined groups from across the country at the National Day of Action on Jobs during President Obama's Jobs Summit. The groups asked the President and Congress to create a community jobs program that would put 2.5 million people to work in jobs with living wages, working to improve their communities.

* One of VOP's interns worked with students in a Social Justice Seminar class at Christopher Newport University. Each of four groups worked on one of VOP's issue campaigns and developed direct actions around their issue, including virtual phone banking, setting up a table on campus, creating a Facebook group, meeting with the campus police chief, and talking with Hampton City Council.

* Four VOP members, an intern, and an organizer served on a panel at the Social Work Celebration of 80 social work students at James Madison University, sharing information on law enforcement training activity and voting rights restoration. The keynote speaker was a VOP member.

* VOP staff and leaders made presentations at national meetings as well, including the Council of Foundations, the Funders Committee for Civic Participation, the Civic Engagement Network, State Voices, and the Western States Center's CSTI training ("Building Statewide Power" and "Applied Analysis: Power Mapping").

* VOP received the 2009 Community Change Champion Award from the Center for Community Change for making a deep and meaningful commitment to low-income communities and disenfranchised constituencies.

* We received the 2009 Mitch Van Yahres Family-Friendly Employer Award from Children, Youth & Family Services in Charlottesville for providing VOP employees full family health care coverage with no out-of-pocket expense, as well as a long list of other family-friendly benefits.

* The Hampton Citizen Unity Commission award was given to VOP for working to improve cultural diversity and race relations.

# 2010

*In 2010, we dropped "Project" from our name – and officially became Virginia Organizing.*

* The Virginia Organizing Chapter at the College of William and Mary helped students register to vote and participated in an anti-discrimination rally to oppose the Virginia Attorney General's letter suggesting the repeal of non-discrimination policies at colleges and universities.

* Students in a University of Virginia Multicultural Education class learned about the legislative process and made more than 10,000 phone calls to encourage people to contact members of Congress on health care reform, while also targeting state legislative districts to find more people who want to be active in their community and asking questions about state budget/revenue issues.

* Virginia Organizing worked with the Providence Mobile Home Park Community to achieve an incredible victory for affordable housing when the Chesapeake City Council voted unanimously to turn down the rezoning application that would have allowed the applicant to displace 170 families and build condo units on the property.

* Virginia Organizing celebrated on March 23, 2010, when the Patient Protection and Affordable Care Act passed.

* Thanks to the work of Virginia Organizing and allied organizations, every jurisdiction west of I-81 in southwest Virginia now has a Drug Court. (There was only one in the region two years before. Even though the state legislature did not provide funding, county governments, re-entry groups, attorneys, and community service boards pitched in staff time to get it done.)

* Virginia Organizing worked with the Mayfield Civic Association on preventing rail cars carrying hazardous waste from parking in residential areas of Fredericksburg.

* Virginia Organizing joined with the Human Rights Commission of Virginia Beach to draft a resolution, which was then adopted by the City Council, that states, "The City of Virginia Beach strives to continue to provide an environment that is

welcoming and protects human rights of all in our community."

* We held Bake Sales for the Budget across the state to send the message that a cuts-only approach to the budget shortfall is irresponsible. With the proceeds, we presented both an over-sized and an actual check to the Governor's office for $921.01.

University of Mary Washington students held a "Bake Sale for the Budget" to raise awareness about cuts Virginia's families faced as a result of the state's regressive tax system. Bake Sales for the Budget were held in communities across Virginia and raised $921.01 that was presented to then-Governor Bob McDonnell to help pay for some of the Commonwealth's needs.

* Virginia Organizing's new Balance Virginia campaign was established to get Virginians involved in budget and revenue issues. Budget/revenue workshops were held in Martinsville, Norfolk, Virginia Beach, Charlottesville, Chesapeake, Danville, Falls Church, and Fredericksburg, calling attention to Virginia's regressive tax structure. Many local officials and some members of the Virginia General Assembly (and some candidates) attended workshops.

* Virginia Organizing held public "budget seesaw" demonstrations in Fredericksburg and Martinsville. Community members used a seesaw to demonstrate that when cuts are made to education or other vital services, without corresponding revenue increases, the whole state gets out of balance.

* Virginia Organizing worked with other groups to successfully push the Virginia General Assembly to pass legislation that established a number of helpful reforms and regulations regarding car title lenders.

* Virginia Organizing and allied organizations met numerous times with the Secretary of the Commonwealth to discuss how to improve the system to restore civil rights, including voting rights, for former felons.

* We joined the March 21 Immigration/Jobs Rally in Washington, D.C., bringing seven buses from South Hampton Roads, one from Martinsville, and one from Charlottesville.

* The Virginia Civic Engagement Table, a coalition of 25 non-partisan groups across the state, held a leadership training for 100 representatives of partner organizations. Virginia Organizing leaders and staff played key roles as speakers and trainers.

* Hundreds of Virginia Organizing supporters worked on non-partisan election and policy efforts including distributing 3,725 get-out-the-vote door hangers, knocking on 2,530 doors, and making 13,293 mobilization calls. More than 11,000 phone banking calls were made on consumer finance reform, health care, jobs, and unemployment.

## 2011

* Virginia Organizing kicked off the Move Our Money USA campaign in Virginia to call on residents to divest from big banks and invest in local banks and credit unions.

* Virginia Organizing made 96 presentations on protecting Social Security at senior centers and nursing homes and generated over 1,000 postcards to Senator Mark Warner.

* A slew of anti-immigrant bills made their way through the Virginia General Assembly and Virginia Organizing joined many other groups to successfully urge state legislators to defeat most of the dangerous bills.

* A Richmond-based Federal Court threw out Virginia Attorney General Ken Cuccinelli's lawsuit against the new health care law and Virginia Organizing was there to speak out every step of the way.

* On two separate occasions, Virginia Organizing leaders made their way to the White House to join the fight for jobs and a payroll tax cut for the middle class.

---

*Virginia Organizing provided support to Maggie Murphy and a local group of volunteers for a 2006 benefit concert for the work of Doctors Without Borders with Darfur refugees, a 2008 benefit concert for the work of Concern Worldwide also in Darfur, and another concert in 2011 for the construction of a primary school by the HOPE for Ariang Foundation, an organization dedicated to providing people in South Sudan with inclusive access to education, opportunities, and resources with a special focus on women and girls.*

---

* Virginia Organizing leaders visited emergency rooms and community health clinics in the Shenandoah Valley to encourage them to have translation services for people who needed it.

* The Richmond Chapter celebrated the first anniversary of the Affordable Care Act by holding a community forum at the General Assembly Building with Congressman Bobby Scott and Joanne Grossi, Regional Director for the U.S. Department of Health and Human Services. The Petersburg Chapter celebrated the first anniversary of the ACA by holding a community forum at Virginia State University with Grossi.

* Virginia Organizing held 25 tax reform workshops and dozens of leadership trainings on dismantling racism, challenging sexism, and understanding the economy and the legislative process.

* Virginia Organizing State Governing Board Vice-chairperson Del McWhorter and Executive Director Joe Szakos wrote an article, "Organizing for the Common Good: The Action is at the State Level," published in the book *Transforming*

*Places: Lessons from Appalachia* (edited by Stephen Fisher and Barbara Ellen Smith, University of Illinois Press) in which they shared many of the lessons Virginia Organizing has learned in organizing in the Appalachian counties.

* The Richmond Chapter co-sponsored two candidate forums with People of Faith for Equality in Virginia at the Gay Community Center of Richmond and at Virginia Commonwealth University.

* From 2011 to 2013, we built a list of 800 small businesses interested in health care reform. We held health care reform trainings for small businesses in Fredericksburg, Norfolk, Richmond, Virginia Beach, and Williamsburg.

* Students from University Alliance for Community Transformation at the University of Massachusetts spent a week in Danville learning about community organizing, canvassing in low-income communities, and inviting residents to a neighborhood meeting. As a part of the Danville Chapter's North Main Hill week of action, the students knocked on about 1,100 doors and recruited more than 30 residents to the neighborhood meeting, several of whom are still involved in 2015.

* Virginia Organizing phone banks produced 36,681 calls about Social Security, health care, jobs and unemployment, and getting out the vote.

* The Richmond Chapter held a Jobs Rally with other groups at a local bridge to highlight the need for infrastructure improvements throughout the state.

* Virginia Organizing saw many local victories this year, including fighting hydrof-racking gas drilling in Washington County, opposing predatory lending in South Hampton Roads, resisting a landfill in Richmond, working to promote people of color in Charlottesville city jobs, approving a Mobile Home Park Protection Policy in Chesapeake (and later Virginia Beach) to provide protection for families in the event of rezoning and displacement, and improving public education in Lee County.

## 2012

* We made more than 125,000 non-partisan get-out-the-vote and issue-education phone bank calls.

* Virginia Organizing was appalled at the extremist social issue agenda presented during the 2012 General Assembly, so we "broke up" with legislators on "Broken Hearts Day" (otherwise known as Valentine's Day) and gave them each an empty box of chocolates!

* Virginia Organizing's State Legislative Coordinator was instrumental in obtaining bipartisan support for legislation that was enacted adding to the Medicaid program coverage for prenatal care for documented immigrant pregnant women during their first five years in the United States.

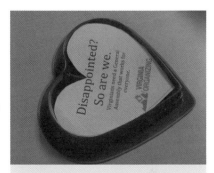

* We took our Divestment campaign to the next level and showed up at a Bank of America shareholder's meeting in Charlotte, NC. Six Virginia Organizing leaders asked the CEO questions to hold the bank, and those in power, accountable for their actions.

Virginia Organizing delivered a box of empty chocolates to each legislator on Valentine's Day 2012 with a note that read, "Disappointed? So are we."

* Virginia Organizing sent leaders to the White House six times during the year. We were invited for special leadership briefings on issues like the economy, budget, health care, women's issues, and the environment.

* Virginia Organizing worked with national groups to raise awareness about the "fiscal cliff" and the budget showdown in Washington. Our Chapters and members asked Virginia Members of Congress to protect and expand social safety net programs and end the tax cuts for the wealthiest 2 percent. We sang adapted Christmas carols at Congressional offices across the state and held demonstrations to support a fair resolution to any budget negotiations.

* The South Hampton Roads Chapter joined the Delta Sigma Theta Sorority, Inc., Missing Voter Project, and the Virginia ACLU in hosting "Democracy's Ghosts: How 5 million Americans have lost the right to vote", a film screening and forum on voter suppression in Virginia past, present, and future.

* The Danville Chapter hosted a community meeting and numerous meetings with local officials about its campaign to lower utility bills and create local jobs through weatherization. Chapter leaders promoted a federally funded low-income rental weatherization program, and the city committed to include weatherization in its rental housing code enforcement. The campaign was successful.

When White House staff asked Virginia Organizing leaders at a meeting in 2012, "How many of you have ever written a letter to the editor about the need for health care reform?", nearly every hand in the crowd of 150 people shot up. Virginia Organizing leaders speak out on the issues that are important to them! (Photo credit: John Erwin)

* Over a dozen University of Massachusetts students opted to spend their spring break with Virginia Organizing learning about community organizing. The students spent the week in Richmond knocking on 1,900 doors, making 1,100 phone calls, and planning a community meeting on local transportation issues.

* Virginia Organizing hired a dozen people to work on non-partisan voter registration drives in Harrisonburg, Waynesboro, Madison County, Southwest Virginia, Richmond, Lynchburg, Charlottesville, Martinsville, and Danville. They visited

high schools, colleges, assisted living facilities, senior centers, and other locations to get eligible voters registered.

* Chapters in the Shenandoah Valley have worked on immigration issues in the community for a long time. They began a listening project to document the voices of the people in the community who are struggling with immigration concerns. In 2012, the Chapters worked to end the partnership between local law enforcement in Rockingham County and Immigration and Customs Enforcement (ICE) that allowed local officers to be deputized as immigration officers. This program, called 287(g), was devastating to immigrant families and communities. What Virginia Organizing found was that 88 percent of those deported under this agreement were deported for low-level offenses such as traffic violations or other civil infractions. The project also found that 287(g) had created a culture of fear among immigrant communities with 70 percent of the participants expressing fear of the police. The Rockingham County Board of Supervisors decided to let the 287(g) agreement expire, a huge victory to the local Chapters and the immigrant community.

* The Danville Chapter of Virginia Organizing peacefully occupied U.S. Representative Robert Hurt's local office. The Chapter members were there as part of a national day of action to tell Representative Hurt to protect people in need instead of giving out tax cuts to millionaires and billionaires. Chapter members handed out flyers, gave speeches on the sidewalk, dressed up in costume, and participated in street theatre to encourage people to call Congress to protect Social Security, Medicaid, and Medicare.

* Students from the College of William and Mary's Branch Out alternative break program spent their spring break in Southside Virginia working with Virginia Organizing. This was the first year of a multi-year relationship that saw Virginia Organizing working with 30 Virginia college students to knock on more than 5,000 doors in Danville and Martinsville.

* The Virginia Interfaith Center for Public Policy presented one of its "Outstanding Service to the Commonwealth as an Outstanding Social Justice Maker" awards to Virginia Organizing leader Mike Stark and organizer Teresa Stanley.

* During the French Revolution, the wealthy became so out of touch with reality that Marie Antoinette was credited with saying, "let them eat cake" if they

have no bread. Congressional leaders were just as out of touch in 2012 and the Fredericksburg Chapter demonstrated this by giving out cake in front of a local art studio on Saturday, December 15, as part of the ongoing campaign to demand that Congress end the tax cuts for the wealthiest 2 percent.

* The South Hampton Roads Chapter delivered more than 100 Social Security stories to U.S. Senator Mark Warner's Norfolk office to ensure that the Senator knows what's at stake with Social Security in the budget negotiations.

## 2013

* The Alliance for Citizenship asked Virginia Organizing to be the lead organization in the Commonwealth for national immigration reform efforts. Our grassroots leaders organized meetings, marches, rallies, vigils, and protests to persuade Congress to pass comprehensive immigration reform with a path to citizenship. A bill was passed in the U.S. Senate that provided increased border security and protections for immigrants, including a path to earned citizenship for the 11 million undocumented neighbors in the U.S. Unfortunately, this bill was not taken up by the U.S. House of Representatives.

Virginia Organizing leaders joined with other groups to protest former U.S. House of Representatives Majority Leader Eric Cantor's obstruction of comprehensive immigration reform legislation.

* We made 65,197 phone bank calls encouraging people to call their Member of Congress and other elected officials on issues like immigration reform, tax fairness, and Medicaid expansion.

* Virginia Organizing sent 5,890 postcards to Members of Congress supporting comprehensive immigration reform with a path to citizenship.

* The Richmond Chapter hosted a community forum with HHS Regional Director Joanne Grossi to share information about the Affordable Care Act enrollment process, the benefits of the law and the requirements health insurance providers must follow under the Affordable Care Act. Virginia Organizing also supported other community forums in the Richmond region explaining Medicaid Expansion, the Medicaid Gap, and other questions about Virginia's implementation of the Affordable Care Act.

* Virginia Organizing supported legislation allowing children receiving kinship care from an adult relative to enroll in the school division where the relative providing care resides. This legislation passed during the 2013 General Assembly session.

* Virginia Organizing worked with other groups to hold a Medicaid Expansion forum in state Senate District 10 (Chesterfield County).

* South Hampton Roads leaders hosted 40 local documentary screenings of "The Dream is Now" to educate the community about comprehensive immigration reform and move people to action.

* Virginia Organizing leaders attended four of Senator Mark Warner's Roundtables on immigration reform and participated in several community dialogues with his staff.

* The Richmond Chapter partnered with the Richmond Peace Education Center for a tax day action highlighting the need to support domestic support systems, schools, public transit, and military family needs.

* In Lee County, where Virginia Organizing's first chapter was organized, 200 people gathered in November to better understand the closure of a local hospital that was vital to the community. The hospital closed due in part to Virginia's

failure to expand Medicaid in the face of decreasing government reimbursements. The forum provided information to local residents and meetings were set up with Virginia elected officials as a result.

* Virginia Organizing held an immigration rally at U.S. Representative Eric Cantor's office in Glen Allen supporting the need for comprehensive immigration reform. Leaders went into the Congressman's office to request a face-to-face meeting with Congressman Cantor.

* The Petersburg Chapter collected over 500 signatures for the "Save Our Route" campaign that the members presented to the Petersburg City Council. As a result, the city of Petersburg chose not to cancel the Hopewell-Petersburg bus route that was facing discontinuation.

* In Danville, the Chapter celebrated a year of success with a focus on local issues like discriminatory policing, downtown development, and fair housing.

* U.S. Representative Luis Gutierrez spoke to more than 400 people in downtown Harrisonburg to support immigration reform in August. In October, the Chapters held a "March for Dignity and Respect" that included 150 people, led by a high school student and local Chapter member.

* The South Hampton Roads Chapter started a monthly tradition in Virginia Beach to stand up for immigration reform – a vigil called "Light the Way" – which was held for 24 straight months. Chapter members and other local activists gathered on the first of every month to stand in solidarity for real immigration reform. These gatherings and other local meetings generated hundreds of phone calls, letters, postcards, meetings, and other communications to U.S. Representative Scott Rigell from his constituents.

* The Charlottesville/Albemarle Chapter supported a successful effort as the Charlottesville City Council established a Human Rights Commission.

* Church Women United, United Nations Office awarded the Social Activist in Human Rights recognition to Virginia Organizing organizer Teresa Stanley.

* In conjunction with the Alliance for Citizenship and other groups, Virginia Organizing held an immigration action outside a fundraising breakfast for U.S.

Representative Eric Cantor at the Richmond Convention Center.

* Students from the University of Massachusetts "UACT" program worked with the Fredericksburg Chapter to move community members to action in support of the local mural project (to update the Spotsylvania County meeting room mural to include African-American and Native American contributions to the county), as well as protecting and strengthening Social Security. They learned basic community organizing methods as they knocked on 751 doors, made 561 phone calls, and had a total of 218 conversations with local residents, which led to more than 50 people taking action.

* The South Hampton Roads Chapter worked hard on passage of a local referendum in Virginia Beach to pursue all reasonable measures for expansion of Light Rail and investment in a regional transit system. The South Hampton Roads Chapter also had successful campaigns to establish affordable single room occupancy housing units built by Virginia Supportive Housing in Chesapeake, Norfolk, Portsmouth, and Virginia Beach.

* Virginia Organizing focused on Medicaid expansion as a key issue throughout the year as part of our ongoing work on health care. The 2013 General Assembly created the Medicaid Innovation and Reform Commission (MIRC) to "review, recommend and approve innovation and reform proposals affecting the Virginia Medicaid and Family Access to Medical Insurance Security (FAMIS) programs, including the eligibility and financing for proposals...". Virginia Organizing leaders attended every MIRC meeting, met with their legislators, wrote letters to the editor, and submitted op-eds to local papers across Virginia (many of which were published), held educational forums on health care and Medicaid expansion, and organized various direct actions to support expansion in Virginia.

* The Petersburg Chapter registered more than 120 students to vote at Petersburg High School.

* We participated in the Strong Kids, Strong Virginia campaign with other statewide organizations to make sure that public officials paid attention to the issues that matter most to children in our state.

* The police escorted Virginia Organizing leaders out of Rep. Eric Cantor's district office. After months and months of e-mails, phone calls, faxes, and visiting his

D.C. office to ask for a meeting about comprehensive immigration reform, we decided to go to his Glen Allen district office, to once again ask for a date, time and place for a meeting. The staff there refused to give us one, then we refused to leave, so they called the police.

* Virginia Organizing had been working for more than 15 years to make the restoration of civil rights process for former felons automatic. In 2013, Governor Bob McDonnell created a more streamlined process for restoration that standardized the process. Virginia Organizing representatives served on the Governor's workgroup to implement these changes.

* Virginia Organizing Chapters across the state began supporting the Mobile Justice Tour in 2013 (and continued support in 2014). The Mobile Justice Tour connected individuals with voting resources, including restoration of voting rights, and promoted sentencing reform.

## 2014

* "Virginia Organizing had a fantastic 2014," Chairperson Sandra A. Cook wrote in the 2014 Annual Report. "I'm so thrilled with the exciting things we've done this year. Virginia Organizing focused on leadership development and building strategic power. We put pressure on local, state, and national decision-makers to ensure that the voices of the people were being heard, especially those voices that had traditionally gone unheard. We even won awards for our inclusivity and focus on social justice!"

* Equality Virginia recognized Virginia Organizing for being an OUTstanding Virginian working for marriage and LGBT equality.

* In February, Virginia Organizing held one of nine media conferences on the same day across the state to push for Medicaid expansion.

* Legislation has been repeatedly introduced in the Virginia General Assembly to require mandatory drug screening of public assistance recipients. Virginia Organizing joined other organizations in opposing this legislation each year and it has failed to pass each time.

* Students from the University of Massachusetts visited the Petersburg Chapter

to learn more about community organizing. During that time, they knocked on more than 1,300 doors to discuss Medicaid expansion and local issues with residents.

# VIRGINIA ORGANIZING 2014 ACCOMPLISHMENTS

 **ORGANIZED 189 COMMUNITY FORUMS** FOR 2,436 PEOPLE AND 142 DIRECT ACTIONS WITH 2,883 PARTICIPANTS

 **SEVEN DISMANTLING RACISM** WORKSHOPS WITH 406 PARTICIPANTS

 **89 LEGISLATOR MEETINGS** WITH CONSTITUENTS

 **353 LEADERSHIP DEVELOPMENT TRAININGS** WITH 3,675 ATTENDEES, AND **1,375 LEADERS** APPLIED A NEW SKILL IN A PRACTICAL WAY

 **CONSULTED WITH 142 OTHER GROUPS** TO HELP MAKE THEM STRONGER

**REGISTERED 280 VOTERS** AND  **HELPED RETURNING CITIZENS** APPLY TO RESTORE THEIR CIVIL RIGHTS

## WON TWO AWARDS
FOR OUR GRASSROOTS WORK!

EQUALITY VIRGINIA RECOGNIZED US FOR BEING AN **OUTSTANDING VIRGINIAN** WORKING FOR LGBT EQUALITY.

THE VIRGINIA CHAPTER OF THE METHODIST FEDERATION FOR SOCIAL ACTION AWARDED VIRGINIA ORGANIZING THE BISHOP LEONTINE KELLY **SOCIAL JUSTICE AWARD** AT THE 232ND SESSION OF THE VIRGINIA ANNUAL CONFERENCE OF THE METHODIST CHURCH.

 81 MEDIA RELEASES BECAME **292 MEDIA HITS**

 **2,800 INTERN HOURS** COMPLETED THROUGHOUT THE YEAR

MADE MORE THAN **60,000 PHONE BANKING CALLS**

ENCOURAGED LEADERS TO WRITE **240 LETTERS TO EDITORS** 142 WERE PUBLISHED IN LOCAL NEWSPAPERS, INCLUDING FIVE OP-EDS

 **1,516 MEETINGS** WITH INDIVIDUALS ABOUT VIRGINIA ORGANIZING

 **RECRUITED 1,990** NEWLY INVOLVED PEOPLE

South Hampton Roads Chapter leaders volunteered to help people sign up on the Health Insurance Marketplace website to get insurance under the Affordable Care Act (ACA).

* Health and Awareness Inc. presented The Community Caregiver hero award to the Virginia Organizing South Hampton Roads Chapter for extraordinary service.

* The Richmond Chapter hosted a local stop of Freedom Riders for Voting Rights and the Caravan for Democracy to support voting rights in response to the U.S. Supreme Court decision that dismantled a key part of the Voting Rights Act.

* The Fredericksburg Chapter held a workshop at the Haynesville Correctional Center to discuss reentry to society, the restoration of civil rights process, and the "ban the box" campaign. The main presenters for the workshop were individuals from the Fredericksburg area who were formerly incarcerated.

* Virginia Organizing leaders, staff, and board members met for the 10th Annual Power Analysis Weekend to discuss power in the state and to develop strategies for moving forward on issue campaigns. Leaders from all parts of Virginia attended the weekend meeting and worked together to explore new ideas.

* Washington County Chapter leaders successfully fought off hydrofracking in the county for four years. After a maneuver from hydrofracking supporters in mid-2014, the county position changed to allow hydrofracking and natural gas extraction. The Chapter raised awareness and fought hard to protect the environment and resources in the county because of the potential for harm to the environment, including contamination of drinking and ground water that could pose serious health risks to residents. Once it was clear hydrofracking would take place in the county, the Chapter began working with residents to do water testing to ensure a baseline measurement of contaminants in the water before hydrofracking, in the event the county's water becomes damaged.

* The Richmond Chapter worked with housing and homelessness allies to save more than 100 units of affordable housing in Rudd's Trailer Park from being condemned by overzealous city inspectors. The trailer park had many problems

that the owners were unwilling to fix.

* More than 250 people showed up to support Medicaid expansion in Charlottesville at a local town hall meeting.

* Virginia Attorney General Mark Herring issued an opinion that allows universities to charge in-state tuition rates for students granted Deferred Action for Childhood Arrivals (DACA) status who otherwise meet Virginia residency requirements. Virginia Organizing had worked with a host of other organizations on this issue for several years.

* Leaders in Pennington Gap, Staunton, Virginia Beach, Charlottesville, Martinsville, and Richmond gathered for one of six Medicaid expansion vigils that Virginia Organizing led across the state.

* The Keep the Ban Coalition presented a recognition for steadfast support for Virginia's ban on uranium mining to the Virginia Organizing South Hampton Roads Chapter.

* While Virginia Organizing focused much time and energy on leadership development and building local Chapters, we also took action to a new level in Washington, D.C., when five of our leaders, including two State Governing Board members, were arrested at House Speaker John Boehner's office for standing with immigrant youth for comprehensive immigration reform.

* Virginia Organizing Chapters in Charlottesville, Danville, Fredericksburg, Martinsville, Norfolk, Portsmouth, and Virginia Beach claimed victories in "ban the box" campaigns by getting their local governments to stop asking about conviction history on job applications.

* The Petersburg Chapter held a Peace Walk that drew a large crowd and made the front page of the local paper. Residents marched downtown and gathered to remember victims of violence in the community.

* Virginia Organizing made more than 60,000 phone banking calls this year. We are the only organization in the state to run a year-round phone bank, using leaders, members, interns, community service volunteers, and people in job training programs.

* Virginia Organizing partnered with the Center for Community Change to host a training on protecting and strengthening Social Security. Leaders from Washington, D.C., North Carolina, Louisiana, and Virginia participated in the training.

* Virginia Organizing spent many years pushing for changes in the process for former felons to get their rights back. Governor Terry McAuliffe announced major changes to Virginia's restoration of rights process that reduce waiting times, remove drug charges from the list of violent felonies, and streamline the application process.

* The South Hampton Roads Chapter honored the Virginia Beach Department of Health for its work in partnering with Virginia Organizing to enroll hundreds of local residents in the Health Insurance Marketplace. Numerous volunteers were trained as volunteer certified application counselors to assist people in obtaining affordable health coverage as part of this "one of a kind" community organizing/public health partnership; more than 30 Marketplace education and enrollment sessions were held. Enrollment in the Affordable Care Act programs exceeded expectations and people who fell in the "coverage gap" were encouraged to join in organizing to expand Medicaid in Virginia.

* The Augusta/Staunton/Waynesboro Chapter screened the documentary "We're Not Broke" and held a discussion with a local economics professor about how the U.S. tax system favors big corporations.

* Danville and Martinsville Chapter leaders met with Virginia Senator Bill Stanley to deliver a 50-foot scroll of more than 500 petition signatures in support of Medicaid expansion and discuss the importance of expansion for Southside Virginia.

* Virginia Organizing was presented with the Virginia Chapter of the United Methodist Federation for Social Action's Bishop Leontine Kelly Social Justice Award at the 232nd Session of the Virginia Annual Conference of The Methodist Church for "the incredible social justice work being done across the Commonwealth" by Virginia Organizing Chapters and leaders.

* On July 30, Virginia Organizing leaders marched to the Harrisonburg office of U.S. Representative Bob Goodlatte to deliver a backbone, asking Rep. Goodlatte

to stand up and use his leadership position to push for comprehensive immigration reform.

* Virginia Organizing leaders met with Virginia Secretary of Health and Human Resources Bill Hazel to discuss Medicaid expansion and learn more about what Virginians can do to help bring expansion to the Commonwealth.

* The Fredericksburg Chapter held a General Assembly 101 training to help leaders develop their skills and understand the process for citizen lobbying and lawmaking. The Chapter also worked with the Virginia Student Power Network to help young people get active in their communities. Fredericksburg leaders met with city officials to "ban the box," hosted an income inequality online workshop with the Alliance for a Just Society, delivered a homemade coffin to Speaker of the House of Delegates Bill Howell's office to push for Medicaid expansion, built a candlelight labyrinth for an immigration reform vigil, organized town meetings on community race relations, and began working on a new local campaign to address discipline disparity in the local school system.

* Virginia Organizing leaders from across the Commonwealth gathered at the Blackstone Conference and Retreat Center in Blackstone, Virginia, for the annual Grassroots Gathering. The weekend included a wide range of workshops as well as mass meetings with Lieutenant Governor Ralph Northam and Secretary of the Commonwealth Levar Stoney.

* The South Hampton Roads Chapter helped organize a Medicaid expansion forum hosted by Virginia Senator Lynwood Lewis and Virginia Secretary of Health and Human Resources Bill Hazel.

* In Danville, Chapter leaders helped develop a response to the local coal ash spill in the Dan River, worked with Piedmont Access to Health Services (PATHS) to support Medicaid expansion in Virginia, and worked with Grace and Main Fellowship to organize local tenants fighting for their rights against an unjust landlord. Additionally, they were able to facilitate community dialogue on racial justice by hosting a #BlackLivesMatter seminar.

* After conducting several non-partisan voter registration drives, the Charlottesville/Albemarle Chapter decided to create a monthly clinic to help former felons get their civil rights back.

* Virginia Organizing members in Pittsylvania County hosted a Restoration of Rights Clinic at the Gretna Public Library.

* Virginia Organizing held a General Assembly 101 workshop at First Baptist Church in Louisa County. The workshop used Medicaid expansion and Voter ID legislation as learning tools.

* Virginia Organizing met with the Louisa County voter registrar to discuss community outreach about the voter photo ID and about how to get a photo ID at the registrar's office. The registrar also shared that more people are coming to the office seeking help with restoration of voting rights.

* The Martinsville/Henry County Chapter hosted a group of College of William and Mary students for an alternative spring break experience canvassing neighborhoods and generating calls to state lawmakers on Medicaid expansion. The Chapter delivered petitions to Delegate Les Adams on Medicaid expansion.

Virginia Organizing members participated in the People's Climate March in New York City to support the call for environmental justice and action on renewable energy.

* Virginia Organizing participated in the Climate Change March in New York City. Virginia Organizing also participated in an "echo" event in Charlottesville at the same time.

James Shelton (right) of the Richmond Chapter spoke with Greater Richmond Transit Company (GRTC) customer "G" Harris about his bus riding experience and how that experience could be improved.

* Richmond Chapter leaders have been active for years in reforming the transit system in their community. In 2010, Montigue Magruder and Scott Burger joined a city task force on bus transit. The task force had been formed with the expectation that it would recommend lowering support for transit in Richmond, but because of Magruder and Burger's voices as transit riders, the task force ended up making recommendations to improve the system. Over the years, the Chapter has worked to push for implementation of the task force's recommendations. Because of this organizing, several of the original recommendations have been implemented, including a new bus pass system and improved signage at bus stops.

* Virginia Organizing leaders across the Commonwealth launched a massive call-in campaign that generated hundreds of phone calls to Virginia Attorney General Mark Herring. Later, several leaders met with the Virginia Attorney General to ask him to protect the civil rights of immigrants being held past the time of

their eligible release by local law enforcement with Immigration and Customs Enforcement (ICE) holds or detainers. This campaign was part of the ongoing work for comprehensive immigration reform, but also had real and immediate implications for people in immigrant communities. The Attorney General eventually issued a favorable opinion.

* Virginia Organizing helped found the Transit Action Team in Richmond to organize an effective campaign to improve bus service in the city.

* Virginia Organizing hosted the Fast4Families national tour in Richmond to share stories and push Congress to pass comprehensive immigration reform legislation with a clear path to citizenship. Fast4Families also made stops in Virginia Beach, Culpeper, Fredericksburg, Dayton, and Harrisonburg.

* Virginia Organizing released an Alliance for a Just Society report on the state of Women's Health in Virginia, which gave Virginia a grade of "C" for current practices.

* Danville Chapter leader Renee Stone was recognized at the Dan River Region Nonprofit Network's End of the Year Celebration as a nominee for Volunteer of the Year. Renee has been active on a variety of community issues, including "ban the box" and Medicaid expansion.

* Virginia Organizing received a generous $1 million gift to fund an organizer position indefinitely. The money was placed in our endowment fund to help secure the future of Virginia Organizing.

* Virginia Organizing worked with several other groups to address climate change and sea level rise in the Eastern part of Virginia. This work will continue to be a focus for Chapters across Virginia as sea levels continue to rise, corporations attempt to extract gas from and build pipelines through the property of Virginians, and other environmental risks remain high. As part of our commitment to environmental justice, we will continue to update our fleet of vehicles to be more environmentally friendly.

* Virginia Organizing met with top officials of Carilion medical facilities to urge them to better serve the transgender community in Roanoke and surrounding areas and they agreed to have designated clinic hours for LGBT patients and

to expand their trainings for nurses regarding the needs of the transgender community.

## 2015 (through August 19)

* The Harrisonburg City Council voted to change the city's hiring policy language to affirmatively state that the city seeks a diverse and inclusive workforce, a key initiative of the Harrisonburg Chapter. Other language was added to the policy to ensure that this goal is considered in hiring decisions for city workers.

In honor of Virginia Organizing's 20th anniversary, Rachel Loughlin designed a logo used during 2015.

* Harold Folley Jr., Virginia Organizing Charlottesville area organizer, received the Ebony Social Club's High Achievement Award.

* In recognition of Virginia Organizing's 20th anniversary, U.S. Senator Mark Warner wrote a commemorating statement in the January 12, 2015 edition of the *Congressional Record* and the Virginia General Assembly passed Senate Joint Resolution #306 to acknowledge Virginia Organizing's service to the people of the Commonwealth. Local governments in Albemarle County, Arlington County, Bland County, Bristol, Charlottesville, Chesapeake, Danville, Harrisonburg, Louisa County, Martinsville, Norfolk, Portsmouth, Staunton, Virginia Beach, Williamsburg, and Wytheville also issued proclamations honoring the work of Virginia Organizing.

* Chapters in Fredericksburg, Danville, Martinsville/Henry County, Harrisonburg, Richmond, and South Hampton Roads held Dismantling Racism workshops.

* Throughout the open enrollment period for the Health Insurance Marketplace, the South Hampton Roads Chapter leaders partnered with the local Health Department and volunteered to help residents access health insurance coverage.

* The Fredericksburg Chapter celebrated a local campaign victory when the Spotsylvania County Board of Supervisors decided to update its meeting room mural to include African-American and Native American contributions to the county's history.

* The South Hampton Roads Chapter hosted presentations and workshops on immigration reform, climate change and local flooding, and health care. The Chapter also screened the film *Remote Area Medical* and discussed health care challenges in rural areas of Virginia.

* Virginia Organizing leaders in Charlottesville and Virginia Beach participated in a nationwide video conference organized by the Alliance for a Just Society on overcoming consumer debt. State Governing Board member Debra Grant was a featured story in the conference.

The Fredericksburg Chapter won a local victory when the Spotsylvania County Board Room mural was updated to include people of color who had been important in the history of the county. Fredericksburg Chapter leaders posed with the new mural panels.

* Celebrations for the fifth anniversary of the Affordable Care Act were held in seven locations: Charlottesville, Danville, Fredericksburg, Pennington Gap, Richmond, Virginia Beach, and Waynesboro.

* Chapters in Charlottesville, Fredericksburg, and Martinsville/Henry County held restoration of rights clinics and workshops to help formerly incarcerated individuals apply for civil rights restoration.

* Chapter leaders participated in national trainings, including the Center for Community Change training for organizing on retirement security issues and an organizing workshop for grassroots leaders held by the Alliance for a Just Society in Albany, New York.

* The South Hampton Roads Chapter gathered for the final "Light the Way" vigil outside U.S. Representative Scott Rigell's Virginia Beach office on April Fool's Day. The leaders' message to Representative Rigell was "We're not fooled

by your lack of action on immigration reform." The action happened after Representative Rigell broke a promise to the Chapter leaders that he would ask U.S. House of Representatives leadership for a vote on immigration reform. After the event, as he had promised, Rep. Rigell sent a letter to Majority Leader Kevin McCarthy asking for a vote on several proposed immigration reform measures.

* During 2014 and 2015, the Richmond Chapter provided support to fast food workers and #BlackLivesMatter activists by helping with events held by both groups, including a 300-person march on April 15, 2015.

* After holding two #BlackLivesMatter community strategy sessions, the Danville Chapter met with the City's Chief of Police to discuss concerns that were raised during these conversations. The police chief committed to make the formal complaint process more accessible and transparent, equip officers to redirect youth to an afterschool program, and explore the possibility of tracking racial data on stops and arrests.

* The Danville Chapter participated in a community forum about the coal ash spill in the Dan River.

* Virginia Organizing continued its support for improved public transit in Richmond and, after years of community pressure, the bus system there finally began installing new, informative signs at bus stops.

* The Lee County Chapter continued work at Hospital Authority meetings to gain access to area health care facilities to meet the health care needs of the community.

* Leaders met with the chiefs of staff of U.S. Senators Warner and Kaine on April 20 to discuss ban the box, the school-to-prison pipeline, and Social Security. On the same day they joined the National People's Action Populism 2015 protest against the Trans-Pacific Partnership. Virginia Organizing State Governing Board Treasurer Jay Johnson was a featured speaker at the Populism 2015 conference.

* Virginia Organizing interns helped organize a rally against racism at Radford University.

* The Washington County Chapter held a local power analysis with other area

groups to set goals and guide future work.

* After meeting with a group of formerly incarcerated people from the Charlottesville/Albemarle Chapter about re-entry concerns and difficulties getting jobs, the Mayor of Charlottesville sent a letter to 100 top employers in the Charlottesville area asking them to "ban the box" on employment applications. The Mayor announced his intention to do this at the same meeting where Virginia Organizing was honored with a 20th anniversary proclamation from the City of Charlottesville.

* The Danville Chapter held a workshop with Voices for Virginia's Children to discuss health care needs of children and families. Participants called their elected officials and voiced support for Medicaid expansion and the Children's Health Insurance Program (CHIP); within a few months, Congress had reauthorized and funded CHIP through FY 2017.

* Chapters held creative fundraisers including dance nights, an Adult Easter Egg hunt, yard sales, and more to support the work of Virginia Organizing.

* The Fredericksburg Chapter began work on a new local campaign to disrupt the "school-to-prison pipeline" that sends many youth to the criminal justice system for school disciplinary issues.

* The Petersburg Chapter held the second annual Green Walk. This year's focus was on the Chapter's new local campaign addressing food deserts.

* Students from the University of Massachusetts spent a week learning community organizing skills and knocked on 1,751 doors to talk to people in Norfolk who are directly affected by sea level rise. People in the neighborhoods were invited to attend a "Flood of Voices" event to share their stories and consider joining the South Hampton Roads Environmental Justice Issue Team to work for change.

* Governor Terry McAuliffe signed an Executive Order to "ban the box" on state employment applications. At the urging of Virginia Organizing, he also wrote to the top 10 businesses in Virginia to ask them to "ban the box" in their hiring practices.

* A group of Virginia Organizing leaders attended the Consumer Financial Protection Bureau field hearing on predatory lending in Richmond. Virginia Organizing leaders testified at the hearing.

* The South Hampton Roads Chapter received the Virginia Coastal Climate Champions award from the Chesapeake Climate Action Network for their work on climate change in the area.

* Virginia Organizing entered into a strategic partnership with the ACLU of Virginia to work on women's issues, using a grassroots organizing approach to reducing stigma, increasing conversations about reproductive rights, and working to get more women of color and low-income women involved in the democratic process. Initial events were held in Danville, Waynesboro, and Blacksburg.

Dennis Hairston of Martinsville attended Governor Terry McAuliffe's announcement to "ban the box" on statewide employment applications.

* The Charlottesville office had solar panels installed on the roof, got a new energy efficient heat pump, and energy efficient windows – energy saving measures that reflect the organization's goal of being good environmental and financial stewards.

* The South Hampton Roads Chapter participated in a successful campaign to secure funding for light rail in the area.

* The Charlottesville Chapter hosted ranking U.S. Senate Finance Committee member Bernie Sanders for a Town Hall Meeting to discuss the federal budget and prioritizing families over corporate interests. The event was held at Trinity Episcopal Church in Charlottesville with more than 275 people in attendance.

\* Long-time organizer Cathy Woodson retired from Virginia Organizing on June 1 after 17 years of grassroots organizing in Virginia.

\* Following a commitment made at the 2014 Grassroots Gathering by Secretary of the Commonwealth Levar Stoney to improve the voting rights restoration process, Governor Terry McAuliffe announced that outstanding fines and fees would no longer be a barrier to restoration of civil rights. Members who were directly affected by this policy change were present at the announcement to personally thank the governor.

\* Virginia Organizing was a supporting organization for the first ever gay pride event on Court Square in Harrisonburg on July 25. The Harrisonburg/ Rockingham County Chapter set up a table at the event.

\* Virginia Organizing leaders attended an organizing training in New York with the Alliance for a Just Society and came back with a renewed commitment to engage young people in grassroots efforts for voting rights and working for change in their communities. The leaders developed Virginia Organizing's first regional program "Children for Change" to celebrate 50 years of the Voting Rights Act and strategize to protect and expand voting rights for all Americans.

\* The Danville Chapter, along with other concerned community members and organizations, successfully pushed the Danville City Council to vote to remove the Confederate flag from all government-owned properties.

\* On August 19, 2015, Virginia Organizing celebrated 20 years of grassroots organizing. As we reflect on our accomplishments and lessons learned, we look toward the future with hope because of the great work of our grassroots leaders and members.

*Virginia Organizing wants to express sincere thanks to all the individuals and organizations who worked with us on the achievements listed above. We recognize the contributions of many others in these campaigns!*

# Building Public Relationships: The Cornerstone of Our Approach

By Ellen S. Ryan (February 1996)

MANY PEOPLE HAVE QUESTIONS about the time and effort it takes to conduct one-to-one conversations as an approach to building a community group. Wouldn't it be easier to just put a notice in the paper and see who shows up for the meeting? Wouldn't it be more efficient to just do an opinion poll or needs assessment to find out what issues people care about? Wouldn't it make more sense to just decide what we want to work on and then recruit people to work on it with us? The answers to these questions are both "yes" and "no" and depend on what it is you are trying to do.

If you are working on an immediate, "hot-button" issue in the community, like trying to stop the siting of a toxic landfill, you are likely to get a pretty big turnout at a meeting you announce in the paper, for example. But you are not likely to get from that meeting a broad base of people who are willing to work long-term on community or public issues in general. You are not likely to attract people who are in favor of the landfill, and therefore not likely to seriously consider the merits of their arguments or understand how they are interpreting information about the landfill, or even what information and point of view led them to support the landfill in the first place. You are missing an opportunity to work out divisions within the community itself, or at least have a clear assessment that they cannot be worked out, before getting into a polarized fight with local opposition you hadn't planned on.

Cultivating public relationships through general, individual conversations provides many advantages over both the short term and the long term. Most people do not have many public relationships in the civic sense, and most of those are rather shallow. In modern life, our relationships with other people tend to take one of two forms, either intimate or impersonal. Our close friends, and often our families, are the locus of our intimate relationships. In this circle, we usually find ourselves with people very much like ourselves, with similar lifestyles, attitudes, values, and points of view.

By contrast, our impersonal relationships are very fragmented. They are not characterized so much as relationships with people with whom we disagree, but as relationships with people we really don't know much about and who don't know much about us. There is nothing wrong with this. It is not necessary to share the same point of view with your doctor on anything other than how to approach your personal health care. It is not necessary to work through your different points of view on gun control, or even to be aware that you have different points of view on the issue. It is generally not necessary to invite your doctor to your child's high school graduation or celebrate holidays together, either.

While there is nothing wrong with intimate relationships per se or with impersonal relationships per se, modern life has left us with a great empty gulf between the two. Public relationships, those focused on the general needs of civic life, on determining what the common good is and how to achieve it, have withered away as the time demands of work and family, increasing geographic mobility, and increasing diversity in our society make it more and more difficult to sort out complex issues in a public forum. It is easy enough to take a position for or against a toxic waste dump in your community, but much more difficult to find a solution to toxics in general. This requires not just taking a position, but engaging with many people with various points of view long enough to reach a solution.

Building public relationships through individual conversations is one step in building, rebuilding, or cultivating a public arena. These conversations help both individuals in the conversation to develop themselves as public persons. Over time, it helps to build an appreciation for and competency in the public arena.

## SOME "HOW TO" STEPS IN BUILDING PUBLIC RELATIONSHIPS

The purpose of conducting individual conversations generally is to cultivate public relationships, or public connections, among people. They may be done in connection with building a new civic organization, increasing the membership of an existing organization, or identifying the major challenges and themes faced by a community. The conversations may lead to identifying new members or focusing the mission of a new organization, or they may result in defining a specific issue for an existing organization to work on and a plan for including people or perspectives that might otherwise have been overlooked or left out.

Almost always, no matter what the organizational reason for conducting the conversations, they result in increased leadership capacity among the people conducting the conversations, and increased credibility for the organization. They increase the number of public connections one has in the community, they widen and deepen one's perspective on public life in general and specific issues in particular. They require people to listen and think, and sometimes change or refine their own points of view in the process. Usually, the process is also enjoyable, although not in the same way that having lunch with a close friend is enjoyable, and not in the same way as getting in and out of the doctor's office without a long wait and with a clean bill of health is satisfying, if not enjoyable. Cultivating public relationships is a doorway to the arena of public life, of expanding beyond self-interest and special-interest groups to engage more and more effectively in addressing the major challenges of civic life.

It is the role of the leadership group conducting the conversations to decide how the conversations fit in with the purposes of the group. For example, as a tool in forming a new community group, the conversations should fit into a general timeline for establishing the group:

### THE FIRST FOUR TO TWELVE MONTHS

Each person in the leadership group conducts at least one conversation a week and meets with the leadership group once a month to compare notes on what the group is hearing in the conversations.

### THE NEXT TWO TO THREE MONTHS

People who were listened to and were interested in holding a house meeting are contacted to attend a planning meeting and set up house meetings to hear about the results of the conversation process and get commitments from people to join the new group. House meetings are scheduled and take place. The date for the first organizational meeting is announced at the house meetings.

### THE NEXT MONTH

Founding meeting takes place and first issue campaign begins.

## PREPARING TO CONDUCT THE CONVERSATIONS

In preparing to conduct one-to-one conversations, many people have reservations, and even fears about what they will be doing. Aside from some people's discomfort with the idea of talking to strangers or people they hardly know, there is often some confusion about what the "point" is. "What am I expected to produce?" is a common question.

The most basic "point" is simply to begin or continue to cultivate a public relationship with the person you talk to. For people who are very product-oriented, this can seem like a rather abstract "point." Therefore, it usually helps for a group of people to conduct the conversations over a short period of time and hold a practice session or workshop to go over why and how to do them. Actually having a one-to-one conversation is often the only way to grasp what the point is, and doing the first one during a practice session with other people who will also be conducting conversations is a good place to start.

In a practice session, ask people what they would be concerned about if someone contacted them and asked for an hour of their time to get acquainted and talk about the challenges they see in the local community.

The first concern that usually comes up, particularly in small towns and rural areas, is that of confidentiality:

- "If I talk to you, what are you going to do with the information you get from me?"
- "If I say the biggest problem in town is corruption on the city council, are you going to tell the city council members I said that?"
- In larger cities, a common issue is credibility and security: "Who gave you my phone number and why?"

Other common concerns are:
- "Are you going to ask me for money?"
- "I'm very busy. Are you going to ask me to work on a committee or come to a meeting or join an organization?"
- "If this is a public opinion poll, why can't you just ask me your questions right now over the phone?"

Imagining what questions or reservations you would have if someone asked to have a conversation with you helps you think through the answers in advance and appreciate that the person you are calling might be just as nervous about being called as you are about calling them. In the context of a practice session, the group as a whole can think through the answers to questions like these and even provide an opportunity to practice answering them.

## SETTING UP THE CONVERSATIONS

The leadership group needs to decide together how to set up and conduct the conversations. To start with, the leadership group needs to be diverse, reflecting as much as possible the diversity of the community in which the conversations will be conducted. Try to build a leadership group that reflects the diversity of age, race, class, gender, sexual orientation, disability, newcomers and long-term residents, political points of view, family make-up, religious belief, and occupation in the community. In this way, the leadership group is most likely to have contacts with the various sub-groups in the community, as well as to understand practical concerns these sub-groups might have. (Working people with young children often have little time for meetings and setting up appointments for conversations, for example, so it is often necessary to be creative about setting up times to meet with them).

There are many ways to set up the conversations, and the leadership group should decide what will work best in the local situation. In general, the group will want to talk to as broad a cross-section of people as possible if the purpose of the conversations is to establish a new community organization. One way to do this is to develop a list of all the types of people in the community the group wants to talk to, and then think of particular names of people to talk to in each category. This generally works if the leadership group is fairly diverse itself. If it is not, it will become obvious, as the group tries to think of names of people to talk to in each category, which sub-groups of people the leadership group has little contact with. If, for example, people cannot think of any elderly people to talk to, the group can take a step back and ask who might be able to help with suggestions of elderly people to contact. Asking help from local pastors, people who run Meals on Wheels or senior recreation programs, etc., could help fill in the blanks. You might want to ask such a person to join the leadership group, or simply help you with contacts so that you can find a few older people who would like to join the leadership group and conduct conversations themselves.

The group may also want to talk to elected officials, business leaders, and the heads of various agencies in order to get acquainted and get an overall sense of how people in positions of power in the community see themselves and the challenges in the community. The occasion of forming a new community group can be the best time of all to develop contacts with people in positional power. It is an opportunity to get acquainted with how they think and develop an understanding of the local power structure and how it works. While these conversations can be scheduled at the same time as conversations with residents in general, it makes sense to have a leadership group meeting scheduled to discuss them separately so that the group can begin to develop an analysis together of the power structure in the community.

After putting together a general list of people to talk to, the next step is to decide how to contact them. Again, the best way to do this varies from place to place and person to person, and the leadership group may need to experiment a bit to find what works best. In general, contacting people by phone, letter, or in person are the usual methods of contact. If the leadership group and/or community organization is new in the area, the leadership group might consider getting a short article in the local newspaper that tells a bit about the group and why it intends to conduct the face-to-face conversations in the community. If people in the leadership group are members of organizations and faith communities, they might ask to have an announcement made at meetings or notices put in the newsletters of those groups. This does not mean that the people the group contacts to set up conversations will necessarily have seen any of these notices, although they might, but it is sometimes helpful to tell people that you did have an article in the paper or a notice in the church bulletin. It adds a little credibility to the group, especially when contacting people you do not already know.

At a practice session, it helps to role-play what contacting people to set up an appointment will be like. Members of the group can use this opportunity to practice handling difficulties that may come up. For example, if you plan to contact someone you already know fairly well, you may be concerned that they will not see any point in setting up a specific time to talk to you:

- "I see you twice a week at softball games. Can't we just talk about this at batting practice?"
- "It would be better if I could meet you an hour before or after the game, so that we really have a chance to talk."
- "I can't. I work until just before the games start and I have to race

home afterwards to watch the kids so my wife can go to work."
- "What time do the kids go to bed?"
- "About eight-thirty."
- "What if I stopped by your house at quarter to nine and we just talked until nine-thirty or so?"

People in the leadership group should practice making appointments so that they feel confident and also understand that sometimes it just isn't possible to set up an appointment. Sometimes people just say no. Sometimes people just can't find a mutually convenient time. Sometimes people are critical of the whole idea:
- "The whole world is falling apart. You're not going to do any good going around talking to people or trying to set up another group. It's a waste of time."
- "Sorry you feel that way. If you change your mind, let me know."

It is important to move on to the next person on your list if someone refuses or just can't find a time to talk to you. The point is to talk to as many people as you reasonably can, not to go to great lengths trying to persuade people who are not interested.

## CONDUCTING THE CONVERSATIONS

As a general guideline, the conversation should not take longer than one hour, and it is important to let people you are talking to know that when you set up a time for the conversation. When you actually meet to have the conversation, it is important to restate the time limit when you begin: "As I said on the phone, this will take an hour or less of our time." Then it is important to stick to what you said. There are many reasons for having a clear time limit. The point is to build a public relationship. The conversations are not rambling chats with friends, and they are not impersonal surveys that extract information from people without revealing anything about the person asking the questions, either. In most places, an hour is ample time to actually engage in a mutual exchange, to listen to rather than quiz people, and to share a bit about your own background and concerns. Having a clear time limit allows you to show that you respect both your own time and the time of the person you are talking to.

Because the amount of time for the conversation is limited, the number of questions that you can ask is limited, too. If the group planning to conduct the conversations is convinced that it is absolutely necessary to get the answers to 15 questions from each person they talk to, the group would do better to send out a questionnaire or do a telephone poll instead. There is time to ask three or four questions at most in a one-to-one conversation, and it is a good idea to decide in advance how much time you want to allot for each question.

One standard question that should be included in any first-time conversation really isn't a question at all, but a mutual exchange of life stories in a public, rather than private sense. This does not mean sitting down and asking a relative stranger to reveal his or her life secrets, nor does it mean disclosing your own. The breakdown in the distinctions between public and private speech, with total strangers revealing the most intimate details of their lives on nationally syndicated talk shows like Phil Donahue and Oprah Winfrey and Geraldo, may make you feel queasy about asking people to tell you about themselves. It is important to understand that the person you are talking to may feel queasy, too, or, on the other hand, may be eager to disclose much more personal information than you would ever want to hear. Plan for either response. Our increasingly therapeutic culture has blurred the lines between what is appropriate to say in a support group and what is appropriate to say in public. Part of the "point" of cultivating public relationships is recultivating the distinction.

Practicing various approaches to the standard opening question in a group is helpful. One way to do it is to model what a public disclosure of one's life story is by telling your own story first. "Well, as I said on the phone, I wanted to get to know you a bit and talk to you about challenges you see facing our community. Just to let you know about me a little bit, I was born here but left with my family when I was six because my father got a job in Akron. My grandmother stayed here and I spent most of my summers here, then I went into the Army after high school. Served two years in Vietnam as a medic. Then went to pharmacy school in Norfolk and settled here because I always loved the area and wanted to come back. I work at the drugstore downtown, am married to a woman I met in college who is originally from Chicago, and I have two kids in high school. How about you, are you from here originally?"

Another way is to ask the person about herself or himself first; this is especially appropriate if you already know something about the person. "Well, as I said on the phone, I want to get to know you a little better and ask you some questions about the community. I know I've seen you every Friday at the bank when I deposit my check, and I see your name in the paper all the time about the work you do on the arts council. Did you grow up here?"

In addition to a standard get-acquainted question, you'll probably have time for two or three more, and the group conducting the conversations should discuss what those questions will be. Asking people what the biggest challenges in their own lives are often makes some patterns clear, especially if the group is able to have 30 or 40 conversations a month with a fairly diverse group of people. Asking people what they see as the biggest challenges in the community is another option. Asking them more specific questions like what the strengths and weaknesses of state government are or what they see as the most difficult issues in public education narrows the conversation quite a bit but can be useful if the group is trying to frame an issue campaign.

In the conversations, be sure to let people know what you are planning to do and extend invitations to people who seem to have something to offer to get more involved. For example: "Well, we're in the process of talking to about 120 people over a three-month period. After that, we're writing up a report on what we've heard and we'll be holding small meetings to let people know what the outcome was. That will help us get the word out more. Then we'll convene a general meeting of everyone who's interested in forming a new community organization." Exercise judgment in inviting people to future events, though. If someone seems disinterested to you, or hostile, there is no need to encourage them to get involved in the group.

It is important to acknowledge and thank people for discussing their views, even if you don't agree with them. One "point" of the conversations is not to get into a heated argument over things you disagree about. Again, practice helps. "Well, it has been interesting to hear how strongly you feel about a mandatory death penalty for shoplifting. I don't share your point of view, but I had no idea how clear the statistics are you quoted about the death penalty deterring crime. In fact, I saw report the other day that said the opposite is true. Maybe you can send me a copy of your statistics and I'll send you a copy of mine, just so we each have a full picture of the debate."

After each conversation, be sure to jot down some notes about what the person said. Some leadership groups use forms with blank spaces for each question. It is okay to take notes while you are listening, especially if you have trouble remembering things, but listen attentively rather than writing the entire time the person is talking. It is a good idea to send each person a short note thanking them for their time, and mentioning anything else that is appropriate. ("I will be sure to tell the group that you are interested in holding a house meeting in your neighborhood. We plan to start them in about two months, and you'll get an invitation to the planning session for that.") If note cards seem too formal, a follow-up phone call might do instead, although a call might be better used to actually ask the person to do something.

## THE ROLE OF THE LEADERSHIP GROUP ONCE THE CONVERSATIONS HAVE STARTED

The leadership group needs to decide how many conversations they want to have and over what period of time. For most people, one conversation per week is all they can fit into their schedules, but some people may be in a position to do several over a weekend rather than during the week. Set a group goal. For example, if 10 people agree to have one conversation a week over four weeks, that means the group can hear from 40 people in a month. Over three months, that means the group can have conversations with 120 people.

It is a good idea to set a time for the leadership group to get together about once a month to talk about what they are hearing in the conversations and to make decisions about whether they want to invite any of the people with whom they have talked to join the leadership group, be invited to the first public meeting, or be invited to hold a house meeting or help with research or another project the group is working on.

The leadership group meetings are also a time to identify problems and try to solve them as a group. For example, if the group finds after one month of conversations that no low-income women with children have agreed to talk to them, the leadership group needs to address this gap. Why are the low-income women refusing? Are they giving any particular reason? What other options do you have? Perhaps the Head Start teacher in town would be willing to invite parents to small group meetings where a couple volunteers from the leadership group could meet with them and conduct "small group conversations" instead.

In comparing notes on what they are hearing, the leadership group begins to get a picture of the concerns in the community which will aid in planning for the founding meeting for the whole group. For example, if, after the first month of conversations, 30 of the 40 people you have talked to say that public transportation is their major concern for the community, the leadership group should consider planning a workshop on public transportation for the founding meeting.

The leadership group may also decide to schedule other events in response to what it is hearing in the conversations or simply as the result of the conversations the leadership group is having. For example, the leadership group might invite a guest from another leadership group in another community to a meeting to share what they are doing and learning in the other group. Or the leadership group might schedule a workshop on how to hold a press conference since the group wants to hold a press conference to announce the founding meeting and no one in the group has ever organized one before. While the leadership group is free to plan and schedule other events, it is important not to over-schedule. The main point is to conduct the conversations, analyze them as a group, and move toward the establishment of a new community group. It often makes sense to wait until the conversations are done before scheduling many events. After the conversations are done, the leadership group will have many more contacts than it did when it started, and many more people to work on planning and carrying out events.

The organizing approach of cultivating relationships leads to creativity and a continuous infusion of energy for an organization. It must be very deliberate and viewed as a long-term process. When combined with a sound analysis of the political and economic situation in a community, strategic thinking, and intentional personal growth and learning by the individuals involved, this approach leads to very informed and powerful actions.

# Virginia Organizing State Governing Board Members 1995-2015

Stephen Abercrombie
Edith Ames
Don Ayers
Mark Barker
Marci Barnes*
Sheila Bell-Clifford
Steve Brooks
Gabby Brown
Donetia Brown-Trent
Jill Carson
Susan Chambers
Rosa Chavez
Ed Clark
Rebecca Conyer
Sandra A. Cook*
Patrick Corey
Kimberly Davis
Kerry Eans*
Duane Edwards
Holly Farris
Herman Frederick
Debra Grant
Norka Gonzales
Jason Guard
Patrick Heck
Emily Heule
Janice "Jay" Johnson*

McDonald Johnson
Andy Kegley
Sue Ella Kobak
Carolyn Lamb
Anita Lawrence*
Laura Lawson
Shirley Lesser
Jon Liss
Debra C. Lyons
Dyana Mason
Johnny Mayo
Jojo McDuffe
Markell McPherson
Ladelle "Del" McWhorter
Jodi Mincemoyer
Tenise Monterio
Carol Moore
Margaret Morton
David Muhly
Donna Muhly
Audrey Oliver
Tracey Parker
Cori Parrish
Shireen Parsons
Sorour Payman
Danielle Poux*
Steve Powell

Joe Price
Mary Randolph-Preston
Tonya Rich
Kathy Rowles*
Robert Salyer
Gerry Scardo
Ray Scher
Jim Schuyler
Jim Scott
Margaretta Seay-Bell
Donna Shell
Tom Simpson
Denise Smith
Faye Smith
Sherri Smith
Donna Sully
Dorothy Taylor
Jesse L. Taylor Jr.
Kristen Tilley
Gene Tweedy
Maura Ubinger
Jamie M. Vaughan
David Walker
Kristi Wallace
Karen Waters
Debra Whitaker
Patricia White

Janie Williams
Kristy Williams
Reginald Williams
Ken Willis
Thomasine Wilson
Helen Witt
Christina Wulf


*served as Chairperson*